Majestic
HORSE

NOBILITY, BEAUTY, AND SPIRIT

Majestic
HORSE

NOBILITY, BEAUTY, AND SPIRIT

Seraphina Alexander

CHARTWELL
BOOKS

This edition published in 2019 by Chartwell Books
an imprint of The Quarto Group
142 West 36th Street, 4th Floor
New York, NY 10018
USA

10 9 8 7 6 5 4 3 2 1

ISBN-13: 978-0-7858-3699-5

Library of Congress Cataloging-in-Publication Data

Names: Alexander, Seraphina, author.
Title: Majestic horse : nobility, beauty, and spirit / Seraphina Alexander.
Description: New York, NY : Chartwell Books, 2020. | Includes index.
Identifiers: LCCN 2019015220 | ISBN 9780785836995
Subjects: LCSH: Horses.
Classification: LCC SF285 .A6235 2020 | DDC 636.1--dc23 LC record available at https://lccn.loc.gov/2019015220

All images in this book are supplied by Shutterstock.com

Front and back cover: Shutterstock.com

PRINTED IN CHINA

CONTENTS

Introduction

Throughout history, the horse has always been an inspiration to mankind and his natural companion. Horses are free in spirit, strong, and energetic; qualities that for thousands of years, we have come to rely on. From ancient times, the horse has served us in times of war, transported us all over the country, and worked in agriculture, pulling plows, to help provide us with food. Furthermore, during their roles as faithful workers, the horse's wonderful nature, loyalty, and temperament has touched the hearts of all those who have come into contact with them. They have a natural grace that can enchant anyone, even those who are not so used to being in the company of animals. In fact, there is no other animal on the planet as beautiful and majestic as the horse, and there are no amounts of words or descriptions that can describe his virtues.

Today, the horses of our modern world are just as worshipped and appreciated as they were in the past. However, their roles have changed from one of work to one of mainly competition and leisure. They have evolved into supreme athletes, capable of physical feats that would seem impossible for a man or another animal to do. Their stamina, strength, intelligence, and unquestionable loyalty have come to provide us with endless fascination. We cherish the joy and emotion that they bring.

Despite thousands of years of domestication and our relationship with them, horses are still endowed with the free and wild spirit of their ancestors who once roamed the globe. They have an overwhelming desire for freedom, they love to be in open spaces, and still display the strong herding instincts that keep them together—even the most cool-headed horses detest being alone. The domesticated horse is used to our love and care and is dependent on us for his welfare. A wild horse, however, is a totally different being, capable of living independently in the wilderness, without the help of humans. Even though they are wild and can't be handled or ridden, they are still just as interesting to love and admire as our stable-kept friends. Watching horses in the wild, just being themselves, is a truly wonderful experience.

This beautifully photographed and inspiring book provides a treasury of interesting information about just how important and valuable horses are. From the lovable and tiny American Shetland to the noble and fantastical Friesian, you'll discover all the interesting breeds from around the world, as well as the awe-inspiring wild ones. In work, rest, and play, some of the most beautiful horses in the world are featured here.

Chapter One
COLORS

The first horses to roam the wildernesses of the world would have been a dull shade of brown, allowing them to blend in with their surroundings, concealing themselves from potential predators. Todays horses are quite different. Through selective breeding, they now come in a variety of colors, shades, and markings. Breeding horses to produce specific colors is a complicated business and is achieved by mixing various genetic material. This is a tricky process as some color genes also have an effect on temperament and performance. For example, the old saying that chestnuts have a fiery temperament often seems correct. Racehorse breeders tend to favor horses carrying the black gene, present in the bay, and they do seem predominant among the winners.

In the United States and Australia, particularly, selective breeding to produce unusual colors has become commonplace, and horses now come in a striking variety of colors and markings. However, most horses fit into the basic categories listed in this section.

BAY

This is the most widespread color and the favorite color of many horse owners. The coat varies from a light reddish-brown to deep black-brown with black on the lower legs, muzzle, and the tips of the ears, the mane and tail being also black. Bays are a genetically modified form of black. Despite its popularity, only one actual breed has emerged: the Cleveland Bay.

BROWN

This chocolate-colored coat consists of shades of nearly black or brown, which are spread evenly over the body except for the areas around the eyes, the girth, muzzle and flanks, which have a lighter "mealy" appearance. The mane and tail may be liver, reddish-brown, or nearly-black.

CHESTNUT

This is a red coat of any shade, ranging from a light to a dark reddish-brown. Darker colored horses are known as liver chestnuts. Lighter colored examples can be flaxen (these are called sorrels). Non-chestnut parents may have chestnut foals; if both parents are chestnut they will always have progeny that are this color.

DUN

There are four variations on the color known as dun, which can have red, yellow, mouse and blue tinges. All shades are particularly striking. Dun horses have darker markings on the muzzle and legs with the addition of a dorsal stripe which may be black or brown. Several breeds of this color type have been developed, the most common being the Fjord.

GRAY

Gray is a coat color characterized by progressive silvering of the colored hairs of the coat. Grays are born with dark skin which progressively lightens with age, leading to most of them eventually turning white in varying degrees. This is not necessarily a sign of old age and is known as graying out. They come with two different coat patterns, the favorite being dappled grey, which is usually the result of the lightening of the coat of a horse which was born dark gray, known as iron or blue-gray. As the horse's color fades, the dappling remains mainly on the legs. The other type is known as flea-bitten; these grays never turn completely white, but seem to revert instead to the base color they had at birth: for example, some may develop blue, black or red speckles; moreover, injuries such as bites and cuts will also grow over in that color.

MARKINGS

Some horses have more pronounced markings than others such as a blaze, star, star and snip, ermine, socks and stockings. They are a good means of identification as they remain with the horse throughout its lifetime.

BLACK

Black is a relatively uncommon coat color, and it is not uncommon to mistake brown horses or for black. True black horses have dark brown eyes, black skin, and wholly black hair coats without any areas of permanently reddish or brownish hair. This is called a non-fading black, which only fades under extreme conditions, the overall effect being a coat of a metallic, iridescent or bluish shine. When combined with white markings, such as stars or socks, it is particularly striking. Fading black is probably a more common variation: the black color will only be retained if the horse is kept stabled or rugged when exposed to the elements. There may also be fading through sweating, when lighter patches occur under the saddle and girth areas. When the summer coat comes through, the coat will have a black sheen, but never the blue metallic effect of the non-fading type, and during the season will become a reddish-brown in appearance. Breeds selectively bred for their black color for example are the Fell and the Friesian.

SPOTTED

These striking horses are much loved worldwide. Spotting can occur in many breeds but is most common in the Appaloosa; in fact, the breed has given its name to the spotted pattern. Markings vary from colored spots on white, white spots on a base color, or a scattering of small white or colored spots.

PALOMINO

Often considered to be the most beautiful, these horses have beautiful golden coats ranging from pale to dusky tan; they are usually the result of a cremello crossed with a chestnut. However, the breeding of palominos is a complicated business and is more common in the United States where the color originated. Ideally, the mane and tail should be pure white.

CREMELLO

Cremellos are sometimes known as pseudo-albinos. These horses have cream-colored coats which are slightly darker then any white markings present. The eyes are pale blue and glassy in appearance. This color is gaining in popularity, however, it is cremellos do not do so well in hot climates, where strong sunlight can irritate their light-colored eyes. Such horses are also more prone to skin problems. However, in cooler climates they can do much better and their striking appearance is certainly sought-after.

ROAN

Interestingly, this comes in a variety of colors and is composed of a pattern of white hairs over a base color which is only confined to the body, the head and legs remaining in the base color. Unlike grays, the color does not fade, but any nicks or scratches will grow back covered in the base color. They come in three basic types: strawberry roan, which has a chestnut base coat, blue roan which has black, and red roan which has bay. The mane, tail, legs, and muzzle markings will be the same color as the base coat.

PINTO

The basic definition of a pinto horse is any color combined with white. In the United Kingdom, these are known as colored horses; however, there is a huge variety of colors and markings with varying degrees of white and color which have different names. They are highly prized and their appearance is extremely striking. In the United States, pintos are very popular and can be found all over the country. While pinto colored horses are not considered as a "breed," several color breed registries have been established to encourage the breeding and standards of pinto colored horses.

CONFORMATION

When considering the kind of horse you would like, be it Shetland Pony or a Thoroughbred, it is important to understand the rules of conformation which apply to all breeds, as a horse that is well-made will perform well and is far less likely to become unsound.

Study the horse from a distance and from all angles. It should stand square and the overall impression should be of balance, harmony and symmetry. The head should not be too large and should sit neatly on the neck, which should be gently arched, neither too long nor too short, tapering gradually to slightly sloping shoulders. The legs should be straight and clean with a generous amount of bone below the knee and well-developed joints. Looking at the horse from behind, make sure that the hindlegs are level with the forelegs and that the quarters are even. The buttocks should be well-developed and the tail set high, which is important for impulsion and speed. The chest should be broad and deep to facilitate good heart and lung function.

Chapter One
BREEDS

While there is no universally accepted definition of the term "breed," a breed is defined generally as having distinct true-breeding characteristics over a number of generations. A horse breed is a selectively bred population of domesticated horses, often with pedigrees recorded in a breed registry. Once these traits are established the animal becomes known as a "purebred." In most cases, bloodlines of horse breeds are recorded in detail with a breed registry. Stud books are created for developing horse breeds that are not yet fully established. The aim is to use selective breeding to pursue consistent characteristics, while reinforcing their best features at the same time.

Breeds fall into four distinct categories: hotbloods, warmbloods, coldbloods, and ponies. The breed registries are considered the authority as to which category the breed is listed as. There are also a number of "color breed," sport horse, and gaited horse registries for horses with various phenotypes or other traits, which admit any animal fitting a given set of physical characteristics, even if there is little or no evidence of the trait being a true-breeding characteristic.

Other specialty organizations may recognize horses from multiple breeds, such animals are classified as a "type" rather than a "breed." A hunter is a well-known example of a type.

AKHAL-TEKE

Country of Origin: Turkmenistan

Colors: Iridescent chestnut, bay, gray, palomino, black, dun

Height: Approximately 15.2 hh

A national emblem of Turkmenistan, a republic in central Asia which lies between the Caspian Sea and Afghanistan, the Akhal-Teke is believed to be a descendant of the Turkoman or Turkmene, an ancient race of horse thought to have existed thousands of years ago, but now unfortunately extinct. It takes its name from a tribe called the Teke which still inhabits the Akhal oasis in the Karakum desert, close to the borders of Iran, where the horses traditionally live in herds under the watchful eyes of mounted herdsmen. This aristocrat of the desert is long, slim elegance personified,

The Akhal-Teke is a proud and ancient breed, once highly prized as a warhorse.

but even so has a hardy constitution and can go long periods without water. However, it is usually protected in its native environment when heavy rugs are used to cover its back during extremes of heat and cold. They were once hand-fed a high-protein diet, which surprisingly included eggs and mutton fat.

Historically, this "heavenly" horse was prized by such warlords as Alexander the Great, Darius the Mede and Genghis Khan, while Marco Polo praised the Turkoman horse in his Travels. Nowadays, because of their great agility and athleticism, Akhal-Tekes are most often used for racing and endurance events.

Appearance: Interestingly, the Akhal-Teke appears to break almost every rule of good conformation. Its head is carried high on a long, thin neck set at an angle of forty-five degrees to the body, giving it a proud, slightly haughty appearance. It has a fine, elegant head with wide cheeks and a straight or slightly dished nose; the large eyes are bold and expressive. The nostrils are dry and flared and the ears shapely and alert. Although the shoulders are broad and sloping, the chest is quite narrow. The body is fairly short, rounded, and shallow, and the long loins have little definition. The girth is quite narrow, and the very long legs appear disproportionately long to the body, and taper to small hooves.

The Akhal-Teke has an unusually smoothly-flowing and powerful action. The shape of the pasterns is unique to the breed, possibly developed from negotiating sandy desert terrain.

Characteristics: The Akhal-Teke has a strong character and is not known for its easy nature, in fact, quite the reverse. It is willful and rebellious and will benefit from one firm handler which it can learn to trust. It is an intelligent animal which requires careful and sympathetic training; it does not respond well to punishment and may well try to retaliate. Due to its genetic inheritance it is unlikely to flourish cooped up in a stable and must be allowed a predominantly outdoor life, with plenty of space to wander.

The Akhal-Teke has a rather unconventional conformation. However, the overall effect is extremely striking.

AMERICAN MINIATURE HORSE

Country of Origin: U.S.A.

Colors: All color and patterns

Height: Approximately up to 9 hh

Despite its small size, the American Miniature is classified as a small horse; consequently it has all the characteristics of the larger animal. The first true miniature horses appeared in Europe in the 1600s where they were bred as pampered pets for the nobility. Unfortunately, not all miniatures had such a good life and many were used as pit ponies in the coal mines of northern Europe, including the English Midlands. In the 1900s Lady Estella Hope continued the breeding program, and these are the lines that probably made their way to the United States.

Today, the American Miniature Horse is smart, attractive and the product of nearly 400 years of selective breeding. They make excellent all-rounders, especially in children's ridden classes such as showjumping and showing, and are also used for driving. The breed now has a closed stud book managed by the American Miniature Horse Association.

Appearance: The American Miniature Horse should not exceed 34 inches (86 cm) or 9 hh. It should have similar conformation to a large, fine-boned horse such as a

The American Miniature Horse is a scaled down horse and should not be regarded as a pony.

Thoroughbred or Warmblood. The overall impression should be of well-balanced symmetry, accompanied by strength, agility and alertness; essentially, it should have all the appearance of the perfect horse in miniature.

Characteristics: The horse has a kind and affectionate nature. It is also gentle and placid, making it an ideal companion animal. It is excellent for children, and inspires confidence because it is easy to mount and willing to be ridden; its small stature also makes it suitable for the less able. The foals are particularly attractive, ranging from 16–21 inches (41–53 cm) in height.

AMERICAN SADDLEBRED

Country of Origin: U.S.A.

Colors: All the usual solid colors, also palomino and roan

Height: 15–16.1 hh

The American Saddlebred's ancestors were horses used for trotting and pacing. They were shipped over from Europe, particularly Ireland, and the British Isles, in the 1600s. Due to their hardy constitutions they thrived in their new home and their extravagant paces proved most popular. It was through these imports that the Narragansett Pacer was developed, named for the bay of the same name in Rhode Island; the popularity of the breed soon spread along the East Coast.

The Pacer is most unusual in that the feet of one side move one after the other, a trait noticeable in many old breeds originating in Asia and Europe. Moreover, the gait proved far more comfortable than the jolt of the two-time trot. Though now extinct, Narragansett mares were bred with Thoroughbred stallions to produce what was known as the American Horse—an excellent all-rounder—which also retained the ability to learn the pacing gait. These, used in the various breeding programs combining Morgan, Standardbred, and Thoroughbred blood, eventually produced today's Saddlebred.

Today, they are highly prized in the show ring, equally useful in harness and ridden classes, in which they are mainly used; but they are capable of competing in other events and make excellent show jumpers and dressage horses.

The Saddlebred is born with a traditional walk, trot, and canter but has also inherited the ability to learn the slow-stepping gait and also the rack. However, its high-stepping carriage can be falsely encouraged by keeping the feet long and sometimes by building the feet up; in some cases the muscles under the dock are nicked to produce an unnaturally stiff and high tail carriage (this is illegal in most countries). In other cases, it can be fitted with a tail brace when stabled to preserve the high tail-carriage, thus depriving the horse of any comfort when at rest: these practices require extreme modification or preferably banishment if this beautiful horse is to achieve recognition in the broader equestrian world.

Gaits: The Saddlebred's gaits place it apart from other breeds and include the slow gait or running walk, the stepping pace, and the slow rack. The rack is performed when both hooves on either side in turn are lifted almost simultaneously, and all four hooves are off the ground together at certain moments; it is quite spectacular when combined with the horse's high-stepping action.

Appearance: The Saddlebred has a commanding presence and subtle expression of movement. The head is small and narrow, carried high, and it has an alert and intelligent expression accentuated by its fine pricked ears. The eyes are gentle but intelligent and the nose is straight with slightly flared nostrils. The neck is long and elegant and is carried high. The withers are also high and run neatly into the back which is fairly long, as is the barrel-shaped body. The shoulders are narrower at the top than the bottom and sloping to create the trademark fluid action. The tail-carriage is naturally high, joined to flat quarters which flow into strong powerful loins.

Characteristics: The Saddlebred is biddable and easy to train. It is gentle and affectionate, loves people, and enjoys being handled. It is also spirited and proud with a keen intelligence and an alert demeanor. Under saddle, however, it can become excitable.

The American Saddlebred has the ability to move its front and back legs together on each side. This is known as racking. It makes for a very comfortable ride.

AMERICAN SHETLAND

Country of Origin: U.S.A.

Colors: All the usual solid colors, also roan, dun, pinto, and cream

Height: Up to 11.2 hh

The versatile and lovable American Shetland's ancestors were the native ponies of the Shetland Islands, situated off the north coast of Scotland. In 1885, 75 of these ponies were imported to America by Eli Elliot and thrived in spite of the warm humid conditions of the southeastern states where

Pages 22–25: The finely built American Shetland bears little resemblance to its Scottish ancestor, the Shetland Pony.

they were raised, and which led to the formation of the American Shetland Pony Club in 1888.

Today, the American Shetland is nothing like its Scottish ancestor, being lighter in stature with longer, finer legs. This is because the original American Shetlands were bred with small Arab, Thoroughbred, and Hackney breeds, resulting in a small horse rather than a stocky pony.

Nowadays, the breed excels in various driven classes, such as the two-wheeled roadster, four-wheeled buggy, and light sulky. It is also good with children and will happily compete in pony, as well as breed classes, and hunter-pony events. It is ridden in either English or Western tack.

Appearance: The American Shetland possesses all the showy attributes of its small horse ancestors, combined with the strength and workmanlike character of the Shetland Pony. The head is quite long and is more horse-than pony-like; the nose is straight, the ears longish, and the eyes horse-shaped. However, it has retained many of the Shetland characteristics: the mane and high-set tail are furnished with thick, strong hair. The neck is quite short but the legs could be considered overlong, though they remain strong. The hooves retain the strength and shape of the Shetland Pony's.

Characteristics: Having inherited many of the attributes of the horse, the American Shetland has an equable temperament which, combined with its small size, makes it ideal for children to ride. It is reasonably hardy and therefore easy to maintain.

Despite its fine appearance the American Shetland is relatively hardy and makes an excellent children's pony. Its strength and stamina also makes it suitable for driving, for which it is often used.

ANDALUSIAN

Country of Origin: Spain

Colors: Gray and bay coats are most in evidence, but others are accepted by the Andalusian Horse Association. In Spain, according to the studbook, only gray, bay, and black are acceptable.

Height: 15–16.2 hh

Also known as the Pure Spanish Horse, the Andalusian is one of the oldest breeds in the world. There is evidence of this fact in cave paintings, which confirm that horses of this kind were present in the Iberian Peninsular around 5,000 BC.

The Andalusian's lineage stems from the Sorraia Pony, which still exists in Iberia, and the Barb which originated in North Africa, with Arab and Oriental strains. It evolved in the peninsular, most of which was then known as Andalusia, at around the time of the Moorish occupation of 711. The result was a horse with a proud, high, head-carriage, and highly-placed extravagant paces.

It was particularly valued as a warhorse, possessing all the necessary qualities to enable it to perform well in battle. (It is interesting to note that El Cid's mount, *Babieca*, was an Andalusian.) Later, in the sixteenth century, the *conquistadores* brought the horses with them to the Americas where it became the basis of all American breeds.

PAGES 26–29: The Andalusian excels in the maneuvers of haute école *(a stylized form of classical riding), for which it remains famous.*

The Andalusian bloodline is evident in around 80 percent of modern breeds and has had particular influence on the Connemara, native to Ireland, the Lipizzaner of the Balkans, and the Cleveland Bay and Welsh Cob of the British Isles. This also applies to the American breeds which share direct lineage with the Lusitano, Carthusian, and Altér Real.

But this popularity didn't last forever, and in around 1700 the Andalusian's heavy, robust conformation fell out of favor, when lighter, sleeker animals, used for hunting and racing, became more fashionable. The breed suffered even more when a plague and famine almost wiped them out, a few surviving in the Carthusian monasteries of Castello, Jerez, and Seville, where breeding continued from the best of the animals.

Today's horse can still be traced back to these lines, the purest and most beautiful of which are still referred to as *caballos Cartujanos*. The extreme rarity of these animals forced the Spanish government to ban their export for over 100 years, but the embargo was lifted in the 1960s, and Andalusians now enjoy popularity around the world.

Today, the Andalusian is used for bullfighting and display riding, where its power and agility make it eminently suited to intricate movements. They excel at advanced classical dressage and also at show jumping and are also used for general riding and driving. They are often to be seen in hand in the show ring.

Appearance: These muscular horses have great presence and beauty. The neck is heavy with a well-developed crest. The mane is abundant and should be kept long. The head-carriage is noble and high, the forehead wide with expressive, medium-length ears. The eyes are dark-brown and gentle, the nostrils flared, and the jaw is large and well-muscled. The withers are well-rounded and the shoulder long and sloping. The chest is broad, the croup rounded, and the low-set tail is thick and long. The body is rounded and short-coupled, adding to the overall strength. The legs are strong with large joints and the hooves are round and compact.

The Andalusian is famous for its extravagant paces. Movement is elevated and extended, making the horse look as if it were floating. All paces are smooth, showy, and spectacular.

Characteristics: Andalusians are proud and courageous, spirited to ride but with amiable temperaments. They have soft mouths, making them extremely obedient when ridden correctly.

ANGLO-ARAB

Country of Origin: U.K.

Colors: Brown, bay, chestnut, and gray, while black is rare

Height: 14.2–16.1 hh

The Anglo-Arab or Anglo-Arabian is a crossbred that now also has its own status as a horse breed. It derives its name from two of the world's greatest breeds, the Thoroughbred, which is of English (Anglo) origin, and the Arab. In the United Kingdom Anglo-Arab breeding rules are very strict, and only these two breeds can be present.

Anglo-Arabs make superb riding horses and excel in most disciplines, including show jumping, eventing, and dressage. They also do well in riding-horse showing classes where their manes and tails can be plaited, unlike the pure Arab which must be left as it is. The combination of the Thoroughbred's complaisant nature and the strength, stamina, and intelligence of the Arab make an ideal combination. The interesting thing about breeding Anglo-Arabs is that you never know how they are going to turn out: they can be predominantly Arab or Thoroughbred, or a combination of both.

Appearance: Ideally, the Anglo-Arab should have the body of a Thoroughbred and the tail and head-carriage of the Arab, though this can vary; some are also lighter boned than others. The head should have the unmistakable Arab traits with a dished or straight profile, though not as extreme as that of the Arab. The eyes show that it can be spirited on occasions; the nostrils are large and flared. The ears are medium-sized, fine, pointed and expressive. The head-carriage is fairly high with a well-developed crest. The Anglo-Arab should have the good sloping shoulders, deep chest and powerful hindquarters of the Thoroughbred. The tail-carriage can be either high like the Arab or lower as in the Thoroughbred.

Characteristics: Anglo-Arabs are usually affectionate and intelligent. They are also brave and spirited and will always give of their very best.

Anglo-Arabs make versatile all-rounders, excelling at show jumping, dressage, and eventing.

APPALOOSA

Country of Origin: U.S.A. and Europe

Colors and patterns: There are various color permutations, including white with chestnut, bay and black. They can also be one overall color or roan.
Blanket: White over the quarters and loins with a contrasting base color.
Spots: White or dark spots appearing over all or on a portion of the body.
Blanket with spots: A combination of the above.
Roan blanket: Partially roan, usually patterned over the quarters and loins.
Roan blanket with spots: A roan blanket which has spots within it.
Leopard: White with dark spots.
Snowflake: Dominant spotting over the quarters and loins.
Frost: White specks with a dark background.

Height: 14.2–15.2 hh

The Appaloosa is an American breed best known for its colorful spotted coat pattern. The gene which produces the spotted permutation in horses is an ancient one, as indicated by the Cro-Magnon depictions of such horses in caves. For many centuries horses such as these were highly prized in Europe and Asia and are often featured in seventeenth-century Chinese art.

The *conquistadores* introduced the spotted gene to the Americas with stock which they bought with them, then generations of these horses eventually passed to the Nez Perce Native Americans, who inhabited north-east Oregon along the Palouse River. They were probably the first tribe to have selective breeding programs, and adhered to strict guidelines to produce the best stock. It was therefore the Nez Perce who first developed the Appaloosa, said to be America's oldest breed.

Nowadays, the Appaloosa is enjoying renewed popularity: the horse does not have to be spotted but there are three requirements: sclera around the eyeball, striped hooves, and the skin beneath the hair must be mottled.

The Appaloosa is an excellent all-rounder, commonly used in Western events such as roping, cow pony, and barrel racing and looks well in Western tack. They also appear in showing classes, particularly in Britain, such as

riding horse and colored horse, and are also good at cross-country and show jumping.

There are some obvious differences between American and European Appaloosas. The U.S. types have been crossed with Quarter Horses and have developed the size and conformation of this breed. In Europe, Appaloosas are larger and more like warmbloods, making them ideal for jumping and dressage. These are also becoming popular in the United States.

Appearance: This is a workmanlike horse, the head fairly plain with short, tapered ears, the eyes alert and inquisitive with the mandatory white rings or sclera around the edges of the eyeball. The neck and body are compact and well-muscled and the quarters are powerful with well-developed limbs. The tail and mane hair is usually quite sparse. The hooves should be striped.

Characteristics: Appaloosas are great all-rounders: they are good-natured and hardy with plenty of stamina, speed, and agility.

PAGES 32–35: The Appaloosa has long been the popular choice of Native Americans. Today, it is enjoying worldwide popularity.

ARABIAN

Country of Origin: Middle East

Colors: All solid colors are possible, but chestnut and gray are most common

Height: 14–15.2 hh

With a distinctive head shape and high tail-carriage, the Arabian or Arab is one of the most easily recognizable horse breeds in the world. It is one of the oldest of the hotblooded breeds, and its bloodlines are present in many modern breeds of today which extend throughout Europe and the United States. The name is not strictly accurate as the original "Arab" could have been a small Oriental-type wild horse which lived in Eastern Europe, the Near and the Middle East. The Arab was further developed as Islam assimilated the breed and Muslim invaders used it as cavalry. Today's modern Arabians can date their descent from five foundation mares known as Al-Khamesh (The Five), said to have been selected by Mohammed for their obedience.

The Arab was also of great importance to the Bedouin, the nomadic Arabs of the desert, who can trace their association with the breed back to 3000 BC to a mare called Baz and a stallion called Hoshaba. Arab blood is therefore highly effective when mixed with other breeds, and usually brings great improvements to the resulting offspring.

Pages 36–39: The Arabian is an ancient, hotblooded breed that has been used to improve many other breeds, particularly the Thoroughbred.

Arab horses were so-named when they were imported from the Arabian peninsular to Britain in the nineteenth century. The Arab is also the foundation horse for the Thoroughbred.

Arabs are extremely beautiful, with a delicacy that belies their strength and stamina. They shine in riding events such as dressage, riding horse, and in-hand showing. They also excel in disciplines that rely on strength, such as endurance riding and racing. Arabs have the reputation of not being able to jump, which is untrue; they are keen jumpers but lack the ability to compete at high level.

Appearance: The head is short and refined, with a dish-shaped profile and a tapered muzzle with large nostrils. The eyes are large, wide-spaced, and low-set, and the ears small, shapely, and set well apart. The jaw is rounded and forms a curved arch where head and neck meet, known as the *mitbah*.

The back is slightly concave with sloping shoulders and well-defined withers. The croup is level and the girth deep. The tail is set high. The legs are strong, hard, and clean with flat knees, short cannons, and well-defined tendons; the hooves are hard and tough. The Arab also has a distinctive skeletal feature in that it has less vertebrae, i.e., 5 lumbar, 17 rib, and 16 tail, compared with 6-18-18 in other breeds, giving it a short-coupled appearance. The horse's action is as if it were floating on air. Due to their desert origins they have a fine coat and skin which is designed to release heat. Consequently, they require special care in winter, though they are tougher than Thoroughbreds.

Characteristics: Arabs are famous for their intelligence and responsiveness. They are also affectionate and respectful of other animals and human beings, being especially good with children. The reverse side of their character is fiery and courageous; they can also be stubborn if asked to do something against their will.

ARDENNAIS

Country of Origin: France

Colors: The most common color is strawberry roan, with distinctive black points, though any other solid color is acceptable apart from black

Height: 15–16 hh

The Ardennais or Ardennes is one of the oldest breeds of draft horse, and originates from the Ardennes area in Belgium, Luxembourg, and France, though it is regarded as French. A heavy draft horse, it is thought to be descended from the prehistoric Diluvial Horse of Solutré and was highly prized by the Romans, probably evolving into the great warhorse of the Middle Ages. In later centuries it continued to be used as a cavalry horse and was part of Napoleon's invasion of Russia in 1812, its hardiness enabling it to cope with the harsh Russian winters.

The original Ardennais was fairly small, but by breeding it with the much larger Belgian Brabant it increased in size and shape to the horse it is today. By the nineteenth century, further breeds where added, such as Arab, Thoroughbred, French Boulonnais, and Percheron. This resulted in three distinctive types: the old original type which is around 15 hh; the Trait du Nord, which is much larger and heavier; and the Auxois, which is very heavy, and is by far the most removed from the original.

Appearance: The Ardennais is one of the heaviest of the heavy draft type. Unusually, the head is quite fine, the ears are small and wide apart, the eyes are prominent and friendly, and the nose is straight. The neck is quite short, broad, and very strong, as is the back. The legs are short and thick-set.

Characteristics: The Ardennais has been bred to do heavy work, which is evident in all aspects of its conformation. It is good-natured and obedient.

The Ardennais is one of the heavier of the draft breeds. Today, it can still be seen at work in France and Belgium.

AUSTRALIAN STOCK HORSE

Country of Origin: Australia

Colors: Most colors and pinto

Height: 15–16.2 hh

The Australian Stock Horse is a hardy breed noted for its endurance, agility, and good temperament. It has a history that began in the eighteenth century, when horses were imported into Australia from South Africa and Chile. These tended to have excellent constitutions, being descended not only from Iberian, Arab, Barb, Criollo, and Basuto stock, but also from Indonesian ponies. However, the quality of the first horses was said to be not good enough, though later infusions of Arab and Thoroughbred greatly improved the condition of the stock.

The breed, also known as the New South Wales Horse was once important as a cavalry horse, used by the British in India, but soon became popular with stockmen where its soundness and endurance were assets in the huge expanses of the Australian outback; it was also used in harness.

The Australian Stock Horse has been especially bred for Australian conditions and is still valued as a working horse.

By the 1940s the Australian Stock Horse had become a quality horse, but after the Second World War the population was allowed to dwindle. It was bred with other horses which subsequently weakened the breed until it became rather inferior. Today, steps are being taken to improve it by using Quarter Horse, Arab and Thoroughbred, but, as yet, the Waler is not a consistent breed.

Appearance: The ideal Australian Stock Horse has a fine head with a broad forehead, straight nose, and medium-length alert ears. The eyes are kind, inquisitive, and intelligent. The neck is long and elegant with a slight crest, and the shoulders are sloping. The chest is broad with a deep girth, while the body is of medium length with strong loins and well-developed quarters. The legs are strong with shapely hooves.

Characteristics: The Australian Stock Horse has excellent stamina and endurance. It is obedient and willing to work and is kind and intelligent.

BAVARIAN WARMBLOOD

Country of Origin: Germany

Colors: All solid colors

Height: 16.1–16.2 hh

The Bavarian Warmblood is a breed of southern Germany that developed from an older Bavarian heavy warmblood breed called the Rottaler, a heavy horse bred from Norman and Oldenburg stallions. The best Rottalers were calm, substantial horses used for pulling carriages and for agriculture during the Second World War, when it was in great demand.

Today, the Bavarian Warmblood is something of an innovation, composed of Rottaler mixed with Hanoverian, Westphalian, Trakehner, and Thoroughbred bloodlines to produce a much lighter horse.

Appearance: This large elegant horse is similar in stature to the Hanoverian, though of a slightly lesser weight. It has a neat head, thick well-set neck, a heavy chest with a long sloping shoulder, and high withers. The back is fairly long and well-muscled with strong legs and large hocks.

Characteristics: The Bavarian is a good-natured and willing worker. It has been bred to excel in all disciplines, which includes dressage, show jumping and eventing.

The Bavarian Warmblood is the perfect all-round sport horse that excels in dressage, eventing, and show jumping.

BELGIAN WARMBLOOD

Country of Origin: Belgium

Colors: All solid colors

Height: Never deviates between 16.1–16.2 hh

The Belgian Warmblood is a breed registered with the Belgian Warmblood Studbook. It is a relatively new breed, having been developed in the last century. It is the product of the selective breeding of Belgium's finest cavalry horses, as well as heavier breeds used in agriculture. They have been improved with Thoroughbreds and Anglo-Arabs as well as with other already established European warmbloods, such as the Hanoverian, Holstein, Selle Français, and Dutch Warmblood. The result is a quality riding and competition horse which excels in international competition, particularly show jumping, eventing, and dressage. Interestingly, there are strong numbers of Belgian Warmblood show hunters in the United States.

Appearance: The Belgian Warmblood is near perfect in conformation and has many of the Thoroughbred characteristics. The head is of medium size with a straight nose and kind, alert eyes. The neck forms a graceful arch and is long and well-developed. The chest is substantial with a deep girth and sloping shoulder. The back is of medium length with muscular loins and powerful quarters. The legs are strong with large joints and the hooves are well-shaped.

Characteristics: Belgian Warmbloods are much admired for their fluid paces, supple action, and jumping ability. They are spirited and courageous as well as kind and willing.

PAGES 46–49: The Belgium Warmblood was created to be a top competition horse. They are regularly seen at show jumping and dressage competitions.

BOULONNAIS

Country of Origin: France

Colors: Usually gray, with the occasional chestnut

Height: Around 16.3 hh

The Boulonnais, also known as the "White Marble Horse," is a draft horse breed. This ancient breed may have been bred from Numidian horses imported by Julius Caesar's army around 54 BC, which were in evidence along the coast of the Pas-de-Calais prior to the invasion of the British Isles. Then came the Crusades and the Spanish occupation of Flanders when other breeds with Oriental bloodlines, such as the Arab, Barb, and Andalusian, were introduced to the region and bred with the Roman-type horses to produce the original Boulonnais; Mecklenburg blood would later further shape the breed.

The Boulonnais is known as the "thoroughbred" of draft horses because of its elegance, agility, and turn of speed. It is well-known for its spectacular gait which made it popular as a carriage horse; it was also a willing worker in the fields and was even used as a riding horse. It was most famous for a race called *La route du poisson* (The Fish Route) which occurred every two years. It commemorated a time during the seventeenth century when it was used for the rapid transport of freshly caught fish from the English Channel to Paris in less than twenty-four hours.

Appearance: There are two types of Boulonnais: the smaller "fish-cart" horse which was used for the fish transportation and is now very rare and no larger than 15.3 hh. Seen today is the large type, with its large elegant head with wide forehead and slightly Roman nose, inquisitive eyes, wide nostrils and small pricked ears. The neck is thick and muscular with a well-defined crest and a thick mane. The chest is wide with a deep, rounded rib cage. The withers sit deeply into the muscles of the shoulders and back. The back is straight and the legs are solid and strong; unlike many heavy breeds the legs have little hair.

Characteristics: The Boulonnais is energetic, lively, and enjoys work.

For such a large horse, the Boulonnais is prized for its agility and turn of speed.

BRABANT

Country of Origin: Belgium

Colors: Most common is light chestnut with a flaxen mane; also acceptable is red roan, bay, dun, and gray

Height: 16.1–17 hh

The Brabant, or Belgian Heavy Draft comes from the Brabant region of modern Belgium. It is of ancient origin, only slightly more recent than the Ardennais to which it owes part of its lineage: the other part of its inheritance is thought to have stemmed from the Flanders Horse of the eleventh to sixteenth centuries, which in turn is believed to be descended from the ancient horses of the Quaternary period. For centuries Belgian breeders produced their stock by selective breeding, which also included inbreeding.

The Brabant's very existence is a direct result of the geology of the area; the rich heavy soil required a horse with great pulling power and big strong joints to enable it to lift its huge feet out of the thick clods of mud. As a result, three distinct bloodlines emerged 100 years ago which intermingled to create the modern Brabant: the *Gros de la Dendre*, which was muscular and strong with huge legs; the

The Brabant is an ancient draft horse, bred for working in the heavy soil of its native land.

Gris de Nivelles, with good conformation and a certain elegance; and the *Colosse de la Mehaigne*, which was large and had a lively temperament.

Over the centuries, the Brabant has had enormous influence on today's modern breeds, much in the same way as the Arab bloodline has been added to improve existing stock. In the Middle Ages, the horse was imported all over Europe and its bloodlines are present in the German warmbloods. The Russians introduced native breeds to it to produce working horses and its influence is also present in the Shire, Irish Draft, and Clydesdale, to name but a few. Today, Brabants are still part of the foundation stock for the breeding of warmbloods. They now appear throughout the world where they are still used in agricultural work, logging, and as dray horses. They can also be seen in the show ring.

Appearance: The head is fairly square with a straight profile, small pricked ears, and deep-set eyes with a kindly expression. The neck is short and very strong and set high with a large crest. The shoulders are sloping and the chest is wide and deep. The body is short with a well-muscled back and strong quarters. The legs are fairly long and muscular and the hooves are large, rounded, and tough; there is not much feathering present.

Characteristics: The Brabant is an extremely docile animal, to the point that it could almost be described as sluggish. However, it has an equable nature, is obedient, and possesses pulling power equal only to the Shire's, for which it is highly prized. It is a hard worker with plenty of stamina and a strong constitution, requiring relatively little food for its size.

BRANDENBURGER

Country of Origin: Germany

Colors: Predominantly bay

Height: 16.2 hh

In the late eighteenth century a stud at Neustadt was founded and it was here that the Brandenburger was developed. The breeding program resulted in a warmblooded horse that was heavy enough for use on farms but sufficiently elegant to pull carriages.

By the end of the World War II, the breed was reassessed and using Hanoverian and Trakehner stallions the Brandenburger was remodeled into the lighter warmblood sport horse much in demand today. The Brandenburger excels at dressage, show jumping, eventing, and driving.

Appearance: The attractive head is fine and medium-sized, set neatly onto a medium-length, well-formed neck. The back is straight and strong with rather a long croup. The legs are strong, straight, and of medium length.

Characteristics: The Brandenburger is kind and even-tempered; it is also obedient and a willing worker.

The Brandenburger was originally bred to work as a carriage or farm horse. Today, however, it is exclusively a riding or sport horse.

BRETON

Country of Origin: France

Colors: Most common are chestnuts, but roans, bays, and grays are also acceptable

Height: There is a range of sizes from 14.3 hh (Corlay) to 16 hh (Grand Breton)

The Breton was developed in (Bretagne) Brittany, a province in northwest France, from native ancestral stock dating back 4,000 years. The Breton was created through the crossbreeding of many different European and Oriental breeds. In Brittany, the demanding climate and poor-quality land caused local horses to adapt to their environment, resulting in a horse that possessed great strength and durability. The Breton is therefore the result of evolution over hundreds of years and long periods of selection carried out by breeders from old varieties of native horses.

Brittany has a long history of breeding distinguished horses which stretches back to the Middle Ages; in fact, the Breton horse was much prized by military leaders around the time of the Crusades, even though the breed was small at just 14 hh. The Crusaders' Oriental horses, which they brought back with them from the East, were then bred with the Brittany horses to produce two separate strains: the *Sommier*, a slow packhorse, and the *Roussin*, used for riding and as a warhorse. The two types remained popular for centuries, and by the eighteenth century had been crossed with Ardennais, Boulonnais, and Percheron to produce a much larger, stronger animal, which was known as the Grand Breton.

By the nineteenth century infusions of Norfolk Trotter had been introduced along with Hackney to produce a lighter but still substantial animal useful for light draft and military work; when used as a carriage horse it was known as the Postier-Breton. As well as the Grand Breton and the Postier Breton there is another type, the Corlay Breton, developed from crosses with Arab and Thoroughbred and is probably the nearest to the original horse of Brittany, being no bigger than 15 hh.

Appearance: The head is square with a heavy jaw. The ears are small and expressive and the eyes bright and kind. The nose is straight, though slightly dished in the Corlay Breton, and the nostrils are large. The neck is short with a well-developed crest and the short-coupled body is wide and muscular, as is the croup. The shoulders are long and the legs are short and muscular with strong cannon bones.

Characteristics: All three Breton types have an equable nature and are willing workers. They are extremely hardy and have plenty of stamina, making them easy to maintain.

The Breton is probably France's most popular heavy horse, and although the breed standard is relatively new, its history dates back more than a thousand years.

BRITISH WARMBLOOD

Country of Origin: U.K.

Colors: All solid colors, with white on the face and legs acceptable

Height: 15–16.3 hh

The British Warmblood we know today began life in 1977 with the foundation of the British Warmblood Society. The Warmblood breed has been of particular importance to British competition for a very long time and is the result of Thoroughbred crossed with Irish Draft. These make excellent eventers and show jumpers and have been proving their worth since the middle of the twentieth century when equestrian sports began to take off in earnest.

One aspect of equestrianism in which the United Kingdom did not excel was dressage. The sport had long been popular in Europe, where European warmbloods were especially bred for the purpose. However, over the last thirty years or so the discipline had been gaining popularity in the United Kingdom as British riders have become more interested in dressage as a sport. It was necessary for them

The British Warmblood was created to compete with the other warmblooded horses of Europe.

to continue to use European warmbloods, but it was eventually felt that Britain should have a warmblood of her own, which led to the formation of its own society.

The term "warmblood" loosely describes a wide range of breeds from all over Europe, each with its own specific set of criteria. It is generally understood that true warmbloods are of European stock and not the Thoroughbred-Irish cross which is technically a warmblood but not recognized as such.

The British Warmblood is based on various European bloodlines, but so far the breed is not consistent, even though registration of these animals is strictly controlled with only the very best being recognized. Today, the British Warmblood enjoys success in many disciplines.

Appearance: As the British Warmblood breeding program is still in its infancy there is no consistent type. But generally speaking their appearance fits the standards of most European warmbloods.

Characteristics Kind and intelligent, and like most warmbloods they are obedient and enjoyable to ride.

BUDENNY

Country of Origin: Russia

Colors: Budennys are nearly always chestnut, with an iridescent sheen. Bays and browns occasionally appear.

Height: 16 hh

The Budenny, or Budyonny was developed for use as a military horse following the Russian Revolution. It was created by the Russians to fit the basic criteria of a Perfect Russian Horse, a standard which is centuries old. A Russian horse should be an excellent all-rounder, equally at home ridden as pulling a carriage. Development of the breed began in 1921 when the devastation of World War I and the Revolution made it clear that a good cavalry horse was required. The horse was named after Marshal Budenny (1883–1973), who founded the breed.

As a cavalry horse it was obliged to satisfy a number of requirements: it needed enormous stamina, a good turn of speed, and the ability to jump; obedience and an equable nature were also needed, as well as great courage. The breeding program took place at Rostov where there was a military stud. The breed is based on Don and Chernomor mares crossed with Thoroughbred stallions; Chernomors are similar to Dons, though rather lighter. They also introduced Kazakh and Kirgiz blood, though this was not as successful. The breed was eventually recognized and was registered in 1949.

Today, the Budenny is used as a performance horse and in all disciplines including racing, endurance, and show jumping. It is also used in harness.

The Budenny was originally used as a cavalry horse, but today it is used as a general riding and competition horse.

Appearance: The Budenny bears a close resemblance to the Thoroughbred, being tall and powerful with good bone and muscle. The head is medium-sized and sits well on the neck. The nose is straight or slightly concave and the nostrils are wide. The ears are of medium size and the eyes are bold. The neck is long and set high and the withers are also high. The back is fairly short and is inclined to flatten towards the withers. The loins are wide, medium-length and muscular. The croup is usually long. The shoulder is of medium length and sloping. The legs are clean and strong and the hooves well-shaped and hard.

Characteristics: Due to its military breeding, the Budenny has plenty of courage and spirit. It is also obedient and has a good disposition.

CARTHUSIAN

Country of Origin: Spain

Colors: Usually gray, but occasionally chestnut or black

Height: 15–16 hh

The Carthusian horse, or Cartujano is not a distinct breed of horse but rather an offshoot of the Pure Spanish Horse. It is considered to be the purest strain remaining with one of the oldest stud books in the world. The Carthusian shares much of its history with the Andalusian. In the mid-fifteenth century the Carthusian monks of Jerez de la Frontera were bequeathed 10,000 acres (4,000 hectares) of grazing land, which they used for the selective breeding of the highly revered Iberian horses, being determined to preserve the pure Iberian blood. When the monarch insisted on Neapolitan being added to the stock they flatly refused and continued to breed their fine Spanish horses. In 1808–14, Napoleon invaded the peninsular and stole many of the best of the stock. The monks, in an attempt to preserve the breed, rescued the remaining horses and from these few the modern Andalusian emerged, which was fairly heavy, and the Carthusian, which was Iberian mixed with Arab and Barb to produce a lighter breed.

Appearance: The Carthusian is slightly smaller than the Andalusian and not as heavy. The head is broad with a straight, proud profile, and widely-spaced alert ears. It has large intelligent eyes.

Characteristics: Intelligent and good-natured as well as spirited and courageous. Carthusians are easy to handle, complaisant and obedient.

The Carthusian is lesser known than the Andalusian, though no less important.

CLYDESDALE

Country of Origin: U.K.

Colors: Bay, brown, and black. Legs and under the belly can be white

Height: 16.2 hh–17 hh

The Clydesdale is a breed of draft horse named for and derived from the farm horses of Clydesdale, a county in Scotland. The establishment of the breed began in the late-seventh century when Lanarkshire farmers and various dukes of Hamilton supposedly imported Flemish stallions, ancestors of the Brabant, to Scotland. The farmers were skillful breeders and mated them with native heavy draft mares already in existence; over the next 100 years or so, English Shire, Friesian, and Cleveland Bay blood was also added. The result was known as the Clydesdale. The Clydesdale Horse Society was established in 1877, almost a century and a half after the breed first began to evolve.

PAGES 64–67: A couple of hundred years ago it was a common sight for Clydesdales to be seen working farms and hauling loads over great distances. Sadly, their numbers have dwindled, placing them in danger of extinction. Fortunately, their numbers are on the increase. Today, they can seen in the show ring or used for ceremonial purposes, such as pulling wedding carriages.

The breed soon became popular as a general farm horse and also for haulage over long and short distances; Clydesdales could be found in most major cities of Scotland, the North of England, and Northern Ireland, as well as in agricultural areas. In fact, the horse became popular the world over, when considerable numbers were imported to North America, Canada, and Australia.

The Clydesdale differs from most heavy draft horses, which tend to be squat and plain-looking; in fact, with its short-coupled body, long legs, and high head-carriage it looks positively refined.

As with all heavy horses the Clydesdale breed began to decline with the development of motorized transport and reached an even lower ebb in the 1960s and 70s. However, a few families kept the breed going and today numbers have increased though the horse is still classified as "at risk" by the Rare Breeds Society. Today they are highly valued in the show ring as well as in harness and as dray horses, where they take part in displays and are even used to pull wedding carriages.

Appearance: The head is proudly held with medium, well-shaped ears which are pricked and alert; the eyes are kind and intelligent. The nose is slightly Roman and the nostrils large. The neck is long and well-set, with a high crest leading to high withers. The back is slightly concave and short and the quarters are well-developed and powerful. The legs are straight and long with plenty of feathering. The feet are large and require careful shoeing as contracted heels have a tendency to develop.

Characteristics: These charming horses are energetic with an alert, cheerful air. They are even-tempered and enjoy the company of other horses and human beings. They are extremely strong with a lively action and a slight tendency to dish.

COMTOIS

Country of Origin: France

Colors: Chestnut with a flaxen mane and tail, also brown or bay

Height: 14.1–15.1 hh

The Comtois horse is a draft horse that originated in the Jura Mountains. This ancient coldblooded breed which is thought to have been brought to France by the Burgundians, a Germanic people who invaded Gaul in the fifth century and established their kingdom in east-central France, centered on Dijon.

By the sixteenth century, the breed was used to improve Burgundian horses, which gained a good reputation as warhorses in the cavalry of Louis XIV and were also used by Napoleon in his invasion of Russia. In the nineteenth century it was bred with other draft breeds, such as the Boulonnais and Percheron, to produce a heavier horse; by the early twentieth century it was further improved using Ardennais stallions.

Nowadays, the Comtois is also bred in the Massif Central, the Pyrenees, and the Alps, where its stamina and sure-footedness makes it perfectly suited to these mountainous regions. However, it is mainly used for hauling logs and for work in vineyards. It is the second most popular draft breed in France after the Breton.

Appearance: The Comtois is lightly built for a draft horse. The head is large, the eyes alert and intelligent, and the ears small and neat. The neck is short and well-developed and the body is stocky and powerful with a deep girth. The back is long and straight with muscular hindquarters. The legs are short and strong with a small amount of feathering. The mane and tail are full.

Characteristics: The Comtois is very hardy and lives to a ripe old age. It is good-natured, obedient, and hard-working.

The Comtois has plenty of stamina. It is a sure-footed horse making it an asset for use in mountainous conditions.

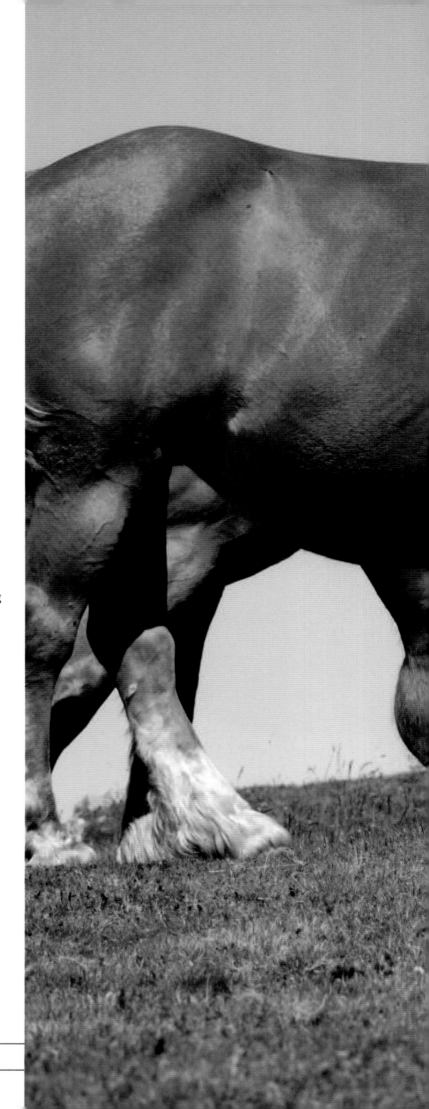

CONNEMARA

Country of Origin: Ireland

Colors: Most commonly gray, but also bay, black, dun and brown

Height: 13–14.2 hh

The Connemara pony originates from the eponymous region in County Galway on Ireland's west coast, a wild area of peatbogs, lakes, mountains, and rugged coastline. Despite being Ireland's only native breed, it is not indigenous to the country. It is thought that it was brought to Ireland 2,500 years ago when the Celts settled in Ireland and brought their ponies with them. The Celts were traders and traveled to and from Mediterranean ports, which makes it likely that their ponies were of Oriental descent, probably Barb. In medieval times these were bred with the Irish Hobeye, which was a much coveted riding horse, famous for its speed, agility, and endurance.

Further blood was added to the breed when the Spanish Armada sunk off the coast of Ireland and Iberian horses swam ashore and mated with native breeds. Later the breed was improved with infusions of other breeds.

The Connemara makes an excellent child's competition pony, particularly as it is a naturally good jumper.

The Connemara's native home is an area of rocky and mountainous terrain with very little vegetation. The weather can be atrocious with piercing winds and driving rain coming in from the Atlantic. Consequently, the Connemara has evolved into an extremely hardy specimen, which is sure-footed and agile and has extraordinary jumping abilities.

Historically, it was used as a draft animal, transporting peat and seaweed as well as taking potatoes and corn to market. Nowadays, it is used for hunting, eventing, showjumping, and driving; it is often crossed with the Thoroughbred to produce an excellent show jumping horse. They can be ridden by both adults and children.

Appearance: The Connemara is a riding pony of excellent quality. The head is fine and set quite high, with small pricked ears, clever eyes, and a straight nose with fairly large nostrils. The neck is of medium length and well-muscled and the shoulders are sloping, with a deep girth, a straight back, and well-developed quarters. The legs are short but elegant and strong with very hard hooves.

Characteristics: The Connemara is intelligent with a calm and kindly disposition. It is an excellent all-rounder and being hardy is easy to maintain.

CRIOLLO

Country of Origin: Argentina

Colors: Most commonly dun with a black mane and tail, an eel stripe down the center of the back, and zebra markings on the legs. Other colors are chestnut, bay, black, roan, gray, pinto, and palomino

Height: 14–15 hh

The Criollo is the native horse of the pampas in South America. The Spanish *conquistadores* were responsible for the existence of the horse in the Americas and what better stock to introduce than the Arab, Barb, and excellent Iberian. It is these three bloodlines which make up the Criollo, the native horse of Argentina. For many hundreds of years it roamed the pampas of Argentina, where extreme conditions of heat and cold resulted in the natural selection of horses that are among the toughest in the world.

The Criollo became the horse of the *gaucho*, or South American cowboy, who quickly recognized its excellent qualities of hardiness, stamina, speed and resilience (they were also used as packhorses).

They are now the subject of a selective breeding program designed to preserve the horse's special features. In Argentina this entails an annual breeders' test in which Criollos travel for 750 miles (1200 km) for fifteen days carrying 242 pounds (110 kg), their only food and drink being what they can forage for themselves *en route*.

Today, herds live in a semi-wild condition on the enormous ranches of South America, where they are caught and broken in as required. They are still used as stock and riding horses.

Appearance: The horse's toughness is apparent from its stocky exterior. The head is broad with wide-set eyes and a slightly dished nose; it has fairly large ears. The neck is well-developed with a wide back and chest and strong quarters. The back is short with sloping shoulders and the short, sturdy legs have plenty of bone.

Characteristics: The Criollo is tough, can survive on next to nothing, and is an obedient worker. It is able to withstand some of the harshest conditions in the world.

A herd of Criollo mares at a stud in Patagonia, Argentina.

DANISH WARMBLOOD

Country of Origin: Denmark

Colors: Bay is most common but all solid colors are acceptable. A little white is allowed on the head and legs

Height: 16.1–16.2 hh

The Danish Warmblood is the modern sport horse breed of Denmark. The story of the Danish Warmblood begins in Holstein which until the mid-nineteenth century was Danish territory and allowed the Danes easy access to German warmblood stock through the Cistercian monasteries of Holstein. For centuries the monks had been breeding the old-style heavy Holstein with highly bred Iberian stallions to produce useful multi-purpose horses; these practices were therefore far from new.

The Royal Frederiksborg Stud, which was founded in 1562 near Copenhagen, was already breeding Andalusians and Neapolitans, and this stock was interbred with a small Danish breed and the larger Jutland Heavy Draft (both coldbloods), with infusions of Turkish and Dutch breeds and later English Thoroughbred added. This created the excellent all-rounder known as the Frederiksborg for which the monks of Holstein had been striving. The stud closed in 1862, but some of the stock survived.

PAGES 74–77: The Danish Warmblood was established in the twentieth century. It is a superb quality sport horse.

By the middle of the twentieth century, the Danes realized that they needed to create a competition sport horse of superb quality to rival other European breeds. Subsequently, they decided to breed the Frederiksborg-Thoroughbred mares with Thoroughbred, Anglo-Norman, Trakehner, Wielkopolski, and Malopolski stallions to create the truly superb Danish Warmblood. It is interesting to note that Hanoverian was not used, which is unusual, as it is present in most other European warmblood breeds.

These horses are the supreme masters of high-level competition, though the less talented still make wonderful all-purpose riding horses. They particularly excel at dressage and show jumping.

Appearance: The conformation of the Danish Warmblood is near-perfect: it has a noble head with large, intelligent eyes, and fairly long, tapered ears. All elements of the body are in perfect proportion, from the long, well-developed neck to the straight well-boned legs and shapely feet.

Characteristics: Admired for its fluid paces and supple action which makes it so popular as a dressage horse, the Danish Warmblood is spirited and courageous but at the same time kind and willing.

DARTMOOR

Country of Origin: U.K.

Colors: Bay and brown with a little white only on the legs and face

Height: 12.2 hh

Dartmoor ponies have inhabited Dartmoor as early as 2000 BC, a fact confirmed by remains excavated on Shaugh Moor. The earliest written reference to the Dartmoor is in the will of Awifold of Credition who died in 1012. The breed stems from the Celtic Pony which then bred with other British natives; later there were additions of Roadster, Welsh Pony, Cob, Arab, and in recent times Thoroughbred.

The Dartmoor pony comes from the county of Devon in the south-west of England and gets its name from the area of wild moorland where it still roams. Standing over 1,000 feet (305 m) above sea level, with wind and rain driving off the sea, it can be an inhospitable place with rocky outcrops and sparse vegetation. Consequently, the pony is extremely hardy and sure-footed and has plenty of stamina.

However, Dartmoors fail to thrive if left solely to their own devices and require hay in the winter, which farmers put out for them. This was confirmed during the World War II when Dartmoor was completely out of bounds. As a result, the population dwindled to only two stallions and twelve mares because of harsh winters without supplementary

The Dartmoor is an excellent child's pony. Its small size makes it easy to manage and handle.

feeding. Nowadays the breed has been greatly improved and with careful monitoring is now flourishing. Children like to ride Dartmoors and they are also used for showing, show jumping, and driving.

Appearance: The Dartmoor has a small, neat head, nicely set, with small, alert ears, and an intelligent and kindly eye. The neck is of medium length and fairly well-developed, as are the back, loins, and quarters. The tail is high-set, the legs are shapely but sturdy, and the hooves are hard.

Characteristics: Dartmoors make excellent children's ponies, and their small size makes them easily manageable. They also have kind and docile natures.

The Dartmoor's most striking feature is that it moves with almost no knee flexion, which produces a long, free-flowing stride similar to that of a horse's and very comfortable for the rider.

DON

Country of Origin: Russia

Colors: The coat has an iridescent sheen. Usually chestnut but can also be bay, brown, black, or gray

Height: Approximately 15.2 hh

The Russian Don is a breed of horse developed in and named after the steppes region of Russia where the Don River flows. It is Russia's most famous breed. It once roamed in herds, surviving the freezing winters and torrid summers with nothing but sparse vegetation for food.

The original steppes breed, known as the Old Don, was bred with various Orientals, such as the Arab, Karabakh, and Turkmene. The Orlov and Thoroughbred were added to improve the Don's conformation and give it incredible stamina and speed.

The horse was the preferred mount of the Don Cossacks, it was also used by the Russian army, and its extreme toughness made it an excellent hunter, particularly in pursuit of wolves. Today, the Don's hardy constitution makes it an excellent endurance horse. It is also used to improve other breeds.

Appearance: The overall picture of the Don is one of strength and robustness. The head is fairly small and neat with a slightly dished or straight nose which clearly indicates its Arab heritage. Ears are small and shapely and the eyes are large and intelligent. The neck is set high and should be arched; however, many have ewe necks. The back is fairly long, straight, and wide with sloping quarters and a straight shoulder. The legs are clean but in some cases can be sickle-hocked. Moreover, the placement of the pelvis restricts movement and causes a stilted action (this fault has largely been bred out). The hooves are well-shaped and hard.

Characteristics: Tough and sturdy with an independent nature. The Don has many qualities which have found their way into other breeds.

The Don, the favorite mount of the Cossacks, originated in the harsh conditions of the Russian steppes. It is extremely hardy and able to withstand extremes of temperature.

DUTCH HEAVY DRAFT

Country of Origin: Netherlands

Colors: Predominantly chestnut and bay, less commonly gray or black

Height: Up to 17 hh

The Dutch Draft was created in the years after World War I by cross-breeding the heavy draft mares of the province of Zeeland with Ardennes and Brabant stock from neighboring Belgium. This relatively new breed was registered in the early twentieth century when the Royal Association of the Netherlands Draft Horse was formed.

These horses were crucial to the prosperity of the farming community where their strength and massive feet made them capable of working heavy soil.

The Dutch Draft is an enormous horse for its height and is still used for heavy work on farms and for pulling brewers' drays. It can also be seen in the show ring.

Until after World War II, it was the most important Dutch horse breed, but with the mechanisation of agriculture, it declined rapidly. Recent surveys show that there are only about 1,400 breeding horses left today.

Appearance: The head is large and square but also quite attractive with a flat forehead and small but gentle eyes. The ears are small and straight, the nose is straight, and the nostrils are large and flaring. The neck is short and well-developed, while the body is short and deep and massively strong. The legs resemble tree trunks with abundant feathering present on the legs.

Characteristics: The Dutch Draft is agile for its size, with a lively gait. It has a long working life and is tough, intelligent, kind, willing, and immensely strong.

Because of its size and strength the Dutch Heavy Draft was popular with farmers, who used it for hauling heavy loads.

DUTCH WARMBLOOD

Country of Origin: Netherlands

Colors: Most commonly bay, but chestnut, gray, pinto, and black are also possible

Height: 16 hh plus

All Dutch Warmblood horses are registered with the Royal Warmblood Studbook of the Netherlands (KWPN). It is a relatively new breed, its stud book having been opened in the Netherlands in 1958. Hugely successful in both show jumping and dressage, the Dutch Warmblood is in demand worldwide as a top-class competition horse.

The Dutch Warmblood differs from most European warmbloods in that it is not based on any breed which existed in slightly different form in previous centuries and which has been improved upon. It contains breeds from all over Europe. The bases of the Dutch Warmblood are the Gelderlander and the heavier Groningen, which have been in existence in the Netherlands since the Middle Ages. The breeds themselves consist of many European strains, the Gelderlander being a combination of Andalusian, Norman, Oldenburg, Hackney, and Thoroughbred, to name but a few. The Groningen was created from Friesian and Oldenburg stock, which was chosen to produce correct conformation, good paces, and a strong presence. A kind and willing nature and a certain amount of hardiness were also valuable traits.

Initially, the Dutch Warmblood was created by mating these two, with Thoroughbred added later to correct remaining conformation faults. Hanoverian and Selle Français were added for level-headedness and acquiescence.

The Dutch Warmblood is probably the most celebrated of the warmblood sport horses, excelling in competition year after year.

Appearance: The Dutch Warmblood is lighter than many warmbloods. The head is attractive, with an intelligent, alert expression in the large, lively eyes and medium-sized pricked ears. The neck is well-set, long, and muscular. The withers are prominent and the back is short and straight with powerful, slightly sloping quarters, and a high-set tail. The shoulders are sloping and the legs are long and well-developed with strong, shapely hooves.

Characteristics: The horse is renowned for its extravagant and elastic paces which make it such a competent performer at dressage and show jumping. It also has a sensible attitude to work with enough spark to perform the actions required of it. Its equable nature makes it amenable, a boon for the less experienced, and its flowing action makes it comfortable to ride.

EXMOOR

Country of Origin: U.K.

Colors: Bay, brown, or dun with black points. There should be the distinctive mealy markings around the eyes, muzzle, and flanks, but with no white whatsoever.

Height: Mares should not exceed 12.2 hh or stallions 12.3 hh

The Exmoor pony is a horse breed native to the British Isles, where they still roam wild on Exmoor, a large area of moorland in Devon and Somerset in southwest England.

The Exmoor is truly ancient, said to have existed before the Ice Age when similar ponies migrated south from Alaska, and where bones that match the modern pony have been found. Exmoor's isolated position has ensured that very little cross-breeding has occurred, which has maintained the purity of the breed; indeed, the Exmoor pony is one of the purest breeds in the world, unlike its cousin, the Dartmoor, which is more accessible and has consequently gone through many changes.

Exmoors are truly wild ponies, though today they are closely monitored, being regarded as a rare breed with only 1,000 ponies worldwide. In the United Kingdom there are approximately 300 breeding mares which produce around 130 foals a year. Half of these mares still live on Exmoor and to protect the purity of the breed each foal is inspected, numbered and branded on its flank, with the society's mark and herd number on the shoulder.

There are also various farms in the area which are involved with the breeding of Exmoors, with the result that

PAGES 86–89: Herds of Exmoor ponies still live wild up on the moor of Exmoor National Park in the U.K. They are closely monitored to ensure the breed's survival.

its future is now looking much brighter. Nowadays, Exmoors are also being bred in other parts of Britain, but all still use the moor ponies as their foundation stock to ensure the purity of the breed.

Appearance: The head is large with a broad forehead and hooded eyes to protect the pony from the elements: this is known as "toad-eyed." The ears are thick and short and the nose straight. The neck is thick and well-developed with a deep chest; the short, fine legs are nevertheless muscular and strong, with a little feathering around the fetlocks. The hooves are small and hard. The coat is dense with a thick, wiry mane and tail.

Characteristics: Exmoors are extremely tough and can live out all year round. If they are to be domesticated, they must be caught and broken in while young. They are good-natured, willing, and obedient and make good children's ponies.

FALABELLA

Country of Origin: Argentina

Colors: All solid colors as well as pinto, gray, roan, and appaloosa markings are also common

Height: No taller than 30 inches (76 cm)

The Falabella miniature horse is one of the smallest breeds of horse in the world. It was created a century ago by the Falabella family at their ranch near Buenos Aires in Argentina. The breed was established by crossing small Thoroughbred and Arab stallions with Shetland Pony mares; then, using selective inbreeding, the Falabella became smaller and smaller to produce the miniature breed as we know it today.

The Falabella is not a pony—it is a miniature horse with all the conformation and character of a horse. However, the conformation of some is not ideal due to too much inbreeding. As they are weak for their size they can only be ridden by the very smallest children. Today, breeders are attempting to rectify their faults and are generally trying to improve the breed.

Falabellas make ideal pets and are most affectionate, and because of their small size are even allowed into peoples' homes.

Although they cannot be ridden, Falabellas are popular in specially allocated in-hand showing classes and are capable of pulling small carts.

Appearance: A Fallabella should resemble a miniature Thoroughbred or Arab, if correctly bred, though some specimens show evidence of their Shetland ancestry. The head is refined and horse-like, with a straight nose and small, flared nostrils. The small ears are wide-apart, and the eyes kind. The body is medium-length with a slim frame and the legs are fine and resemble those of a Thoroughbred.

Characteristics: This is a delightful breed and provides all the pleasures of a larger breed at a much reduced cost as far as land requirements are concerned. However, its constitution is less that robust and it requires the same care that one would give to any finely bred horse. It is amenable, docile, and obedient.

Falabellas are regarded as miniature horses rather than ponies.

FELL

Country of Origin: U.K.

Colors: Pure black with no white markings is the most popular, but bay, gray, and brown are also possible

Height: Up to 14 hh

The Fell is a working breed of mountain and moorland pony originating in the north of England. It is related to the Dales pony. It is a descendant of the Celtic Pony which once roamed much of northern Europe, and which the Romans used as draft animals and in raids against the Picts. They were later used by reivers—cattle-raiders of the Scottish Border country— who required ponies with strength, stamina, and sure-footedness.

Their checkered history continued when they were used by smugglers around the northern coastlines and they were also bred by Cistercian monks who introduced gray ponies, as white stock signified monastic ownership. Over the years, and like the Dales, the breed was improved by mating with other stock, such as the Friesian, to which the Fell bears a resemblance. However, it remains much purer then the Dales which has been subjected to rather more added bloodstock.

Like many native breeds, numbers declined during and after the two world wars, when farms switched to machinery and motorized transport as they became more readily available. However, the Fell remained popular as a riding and driving pony and its fortunes have happily been reversed.

Today, the Fell is an all-round family pony, strong enough to carry an adult and docile enough for children to ride. They make excellent trekking ponies and are therefore popular in the tourist industry. They are also used in harness and the occasional farmer still uses them to herd sheep.

The Fell looks similar to the Friesian—a breed that was used to improve it.

Appearance: The Fell bears a strong resemblance to the Friesian. The head is noble with a broad forehead and a straight or slightly dished, tapering nose with large flaring nostrils. The eyes are proud and intelligent and the ears small and neat. The head sits well on the neck, which is of medium length, strong but not overdeveloped. The shoulders are well-muscled and sloping, ensuring a good smooth action. The body is sturdy with a strong back and deep chest. The legs are strong and muscular with fine feathering present on the backs of the legs; the hooves are well-shaped and are a characteristic blue color.

The mane and tail should not be trimmed but should be left to grow naturally.

Characteristics: The Fell Pony has an excellent constitution and like most mountain and moorland ponies is hardy and able to live out all year round. It is easygoing and enjoys the company of humans beings; however, it is a free spirit and can be willful at times. Fell Ponies are famous for their excellent paces, which make them comfortable to ride. They excel at endurance events and are fast into the bargain, which is an asset in harness.

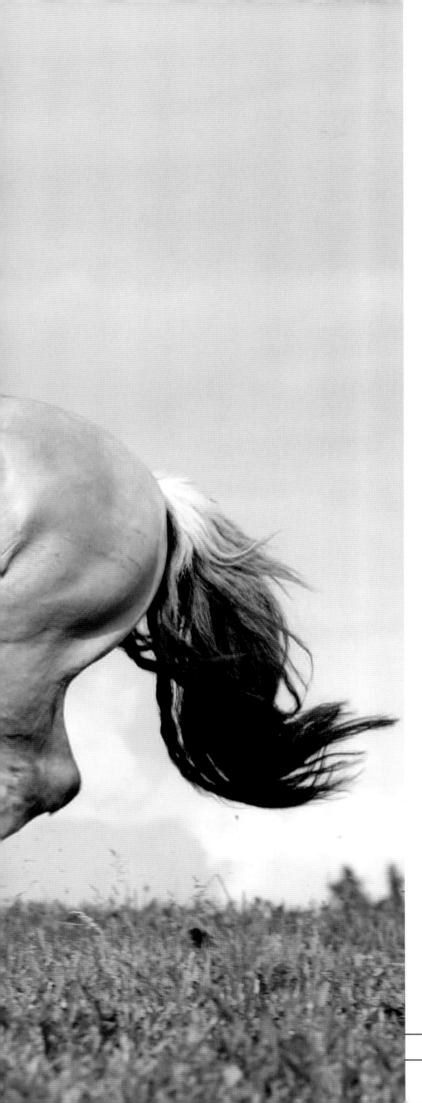

FJORD

Country of Origin: Norway

Colors: Usually a pale gold or dun color, with a black dorsal stripe running from the poll to the tail; this also runs through the center of the mane, the outer sections of which are white. Some also have zebra stripes on the legs

Height: Up to 13.2–14.2 hh

The Fjord horse or Norwegian Fjord Horse is a relatively small but very strong horse breed from the mountainous regions of western Norway. It is likely that the Fjord is descended from the Przewalski or Asiatic Wild Horse, which in turn is descended from the horses of the Ice Age; it seems to have retained much of its ancestors' characteristics, for example, the pale coat, dorsal stripe down the back, and occasional zebra stripes on the legs, typical of the ancient breed. The primitive breed was improved over many hundreds of years by breeding with the Celtic Pony and Tarpan. The result has been used for thousands of years, and there is evidence that it was used in raids and battles, as evidenced by Viking artifacts. The Vikings had a particularly bloodthirsty approach to selection in which they allowed stallions to fight to the death, when the victor became the breeding stallion.

The breed still has its mane clipped in the fashion to be seen on Viking rune stones; the mane is unusual in that it is cream on the outer edges and black in the center, being part of the dorsal stripe. The mane is therefore clipped so that the black part is prominent.

Today, it can be seen over most of Scandinavia, mainly used as children's riding ponies. It is sure-footed and excellent at trekking and long-distance endurance events.

Appearance: The head is attractive, being short and wide with short, neat ears, a slightly dished face, and large nostrils. The eyes are large and kind. The neck is short and thick. The body is sturdy with sloping quarters and a low-set tail. The legs are strong with good bone and the feet are tough and hard.

Characteristics: The Fjord's most striking features are its dorsal stripe and primitive appearance.

The Fjord is most likely the descendant of the Przewalski Horse as its characteristics are similar.

FRENCH ANGLO-ARAB

Country of Origin: France

Colors: Chestnut is the most common; however, all solid colors are acceptable with white allowed on the legs and face

Height: Up to 15.2–16.3 hh

The Anglo-Arab derives its name from two of the world's greatest breeds, the Thoroughbred, which is of English (Anglo) origin and the Arab. The rule for Anglo-Arab breeding is very strict in the United Kingdom, and only these two breeds can be present. However, as this is not a standardized breed the resulting progeny can either resemble the Thoroughbred, the Arab or a little of both.

The French Anglo-Arab is different in that it is a composite breed, originated in the 1830s by a veterinary surgeon called Gayot. It was later developed with the bloodlines of two stallions, an Arab called Massoud and a Turk called Aslan, together with three Thoroughbred mares.

Today, the breeding of a French Anglo-Arab consists of pure-bred Arab, Anglo-Arab, and Thoroughbred. To register a French Anglo-Arab in the stud book the horse must have at least 25 percent Arab and no other blood other then Arab and Thoroughbred going back six generations. The French Anglo-Arab excels in all disciplines, including racing and endurance.

Appearance: This horse exudes quality. The head is small and fine with either a straight or sightly dished nose and a tapering muzzle with fine expressive nostrils. The eyes are kind and intelligent and the ears medium-length, well-shaped, and alert. The head is carried high and sits well on a long shapely neck; the body is medium-length and sinewy with a deep girth, and sloping shoulders. The legs are long, fine, but strong.

Characteristics: This horse combines the Arab's intelligence and beauty with the Thoroughbred's size and speed.

The French Anglo–Arab exudes quality and combines all the excellent traits of the Arabian and Thoroughbred.

FRENCH TROTTER

Country of Origin: France

Colors: All solid colors are available, with the occasional roan. Grays are quite rare

Height: Approximately 16.2 hh

The French Trotter is a French breed of trotting horse bred for racing both ridden and in harness. The first trotting racetrack in France opened in 1839 at Cherbourg and since that date the sport has not looked back. The first races were a means of selecting suitable stallions and became quite an event. The most popular trotters at that time were Norman and Anglo-Norman breeds; later, these were crossed with Norfolk Roadsters from Britain and by the end of the nineteenth century the breed was further enhanced by infusions of British Hackney, Orlov Trotter from Russia, and Thoroughbred. These breeds did much to create a popular and much respected trotter and with the later addition of American Standardbred, which greatly improved it, the breed was considered complete.

In 1906 a stud book was created for French Trotters, though the breed itself wasn't recognized as such until 1922. To be acceptable for registration it was necessary that the horse be able to trot .62 mile (1 km) in 1 minute 42 seconds. This was later extended to include only horses whose parents had both been registered, thus ensuring the purity of the breed. Recently, however, further infusions of Standardbreds have been made to improve the breed and its paces; the result is a world-class trotting horse which even surpasses the Standardbred itself.

Today, it is predominantly used for the sport for which it was bred, both under saddle and in harness; however, French Trotters also make good riding horses and even good jumpers.

The French Trotter has the fine characteristics of the Thoroughbred, with a noble head and beautiful conformation.

Appearance: In appearance, the French Trotter's Thoroughbred ancestry is much in evidence, with a noble head, broad forehead, medium-sized far-apart ears, and kind, intelligent eyes. The nostrils are large and flaring. The neck is long and well-developed with a straight shoulder, deep chest, and well-formed, powerful quarters. The legs are muscular with plenty of bone and well-shaped hooves.

Characteristics: The French Trotter has all the fine characteristics of the Thoroughbred. It has a good turn of speed, plenty of stamina, and a kind and even temperament, though it is not without spirit. The harness horses are usually a little smaller and lighter then the ridden types.

FRIESIAN

Country of Origin: Netherlands

Colors: Black, with only the smallest of white stars permitted on the face

Height: 15–15.2 hh. However, some Friesians have been bred larger, some over 16 hh

The Friesian is a horse breed originating in Friesland, in the Netherlands. The breed is most often recognized by its striking good looks and black coat color. The Friesian is the Netherland's only surviving indigenous breed and is descended from a native breed which roamed Friesland, the western part of the ancient region of Frisia, 3,000 years ago,

PAGES 100–103: The Friesian is an ancient breed dating back 3,000 years, which has gradually been improved to produce the stunning horse of today.

and where the remains of a similar coldblooded horse have been found. As riding horses, the Friesian's history is an ancient one, with evidence that they were used by Roman soldiers when they were building Hadrian's Wall around 150 AD; this is also supported by the fact that Fell and Dales breeds native to the Pennines are also descended from Friesians. Friesian blood is also present in the Orlov Trotter as well as most American trotters.

Over the years the original breed, which was rather heavy and plain, was infused with Oriental and Andalusian blood which improved it to such an extent that during the seventeenth century Friesians were seen along with Spanish horses performing *haute école* and were in demand as elegant carriage horses. During the nineteenth century, however, the Friesian became a rarity, the breed almost exclusively restricted to Friesland, where it was used as a general riding horse and trotter. By the end of World War I the Friesian was in dire peril of extinction, with only three stallions and a few mares still in existence. Thankfully, with careful breeding and an infusion of Oldenburg blood, the Friesian is once again flourishing; today, it is in evidence all over the world, much admired for its noble presence and expressive trot, which is particularly striking in harness. It is still used in *haute école* disciplines.

Appearance: The head is proud and of medium size with small, alert ears which point sightly inwards. The eyes are kindly and expressive. The head-carriage is high and elegant, and the neck of medium length with a high crest. The withers are well-developed, tapering into the back muscles, and the shoulders sloping. The back is of medium length, strong, and straight, leading to well-developed loins and quarters. The legs are clean and strong with slight feathering, and the mane and tail long and luxuriant; when showing, mane and tail should be left untrimmed.

Characteristics: The Friesian has a proud bearing but is nevertheless gentle and amenable if rather energetic.

GIDRÁN

Country of Origin: Hungary

Colors: Chestnut

Height: 16.1–17 hh

An exclusively chestnut Hungarian Anglo-Arab, the Gidrán was developed at the Mezöhegyes State Stud, which was founded by the Habsburg Emperor Joseph II in 1785. This important breeding establishment in Hungary was also responsible for the development of the Nonius in the early nineteenth century and the Furioso from 1885. But in about 1816 it had developed another breed, the Hungarian Anglo-Arab or Gidrán. The Hungarians required a cavalry horse with the stamina, strength and courage of the Arab though rather larger.

The creation of the Gidrán was complicated as there is far more varied blood in its composition than the traditional Anglo-Arab with its varying amounts of Arab and

Thoroughbred. The stud imported an Arab stallion said to have originated from the Siglavy (Seglawi) strain which was called Gidrán Senior. He was mated with various breeds of mare, such as Arab, Turkish, and Spanish-Naples. From these unions seven colts were born which became Mezöhegyes's premier stallions.

In 1820 the Spanish-Naples mare, Arrogante, gave birth to a colt which was named Gidrán II and became the foundation stallion of the breed; today all Gidráns can be

The superb Gidrán has all the attributes of the Anglo-Arab, with enormous presence and elegance.

traced to this one stallion. The breed was developed using Arab, Transylvanian, Spanish, Nonius, and native Hungarian and by 1893 Thoroughbred blood was added to further improve the breed as well as Shagya Arabs Gazal III and Siglavy II, which added more Arab attributes to the breed. The end result was a horse that was very fast, was a good jumper, and had excellent stamina.

Nowadays the Gidrán is used for competition riding and driving, and its excellent breeding makes it suitable for improving other breeds. However, it is now extremely rare with less than 200 Gidráns left in the world, placing it in very real danger of extinction.

Appearance: The Gidrán has all the excellent qualities of the Anglo-Arab. It has a fine intelligent head with a straight or slightly dished face, fine alert ears, and an inquisitive look. The neck is long and beautifully shaped. The body is strong, sturdy, and muscular with long, straight legs. The quarters are powerful, as with all horses capable of great speed.

Characteristics: All the qualities of its noble ancestry are immediately apparent, as well as an impression of strength, power, and vigor. The Gidrán has great courage and willpower which, coupled with agility and intelligence, makes it an excellent competition horse.

GOTLAND

Country of Origin: Sweden

Colors: Black, bay, dun, or chestnut

Height: 11.2–13.2 hh

The Gotland, Russ, or Skogruss is a Swedish pony breed. Sometimes known as the "little horse of the woods," it is an ancient breed, said to be directly descended from the wild Tarpan, and has lived on the island of Gotland in the Baltic Sea for 4–5,000 years, and probably much longer. Due to its isolation, and the commitment of the local inhabitants to keep the breed intact, there has been little or no cross-breeding, and the Gotland has remained largely true to type. The Russ, as some of the locals call it, still lives on the wooded wild moors of the island to this day.

Gotlands were also kept on the mainland, where in 1886 the breed was improved with a Syrian stallion; consequently, their blood is not as pure as their island

The Gotland is robust, energetic, friendly, and intelligent. It make an ideal riding pony for children.

cousins. For centuries they worked on local farms and also became popular in other European countries, where they were exported for use in light haulage and also in mines. Like many native breeds, numbers declined rapidly with the onset of mechanization in the early 1900s. In the 1950s, however, the continuity of the breed was assured when the Swedish Pony Association was formed, set up by the government to protect this unusual and attractive breed, which was further improved with two Welsh stallions.

Today, the breed is flourishing and is used in trotting races and as a general children's riding pony.

Wild Gotlands still roam the moors and forest of Lojsta under the watchful eye of local caretakers.

Appearance: The head is medium-sized with a broad forehead, small pricked ears, a straight nose, and large, clever eyes. The neck is medium-length and well-developed with prominent withers; the back is straight with sloping hindquarters. The full tail is low-set, and the legs are fine but very strong, with small, well-shaped hard feet.

Characteristics: The Gotland is robust and long-lived, with many surviving into their 30s; they are energetic, intelligent and friendly, and make excellent first mounts.

HAFLINGER

Country of Origin: Hungary

Colors: Chestnut, liver, or red

Height: 13.2 –15 hh

The Haflinger is a breed of horse developed in the South Tyrol on the Austrian side of the border with Italy. As borders have changed many times throughout history, making the exact location is impossible to pinpoint. However, the Haflinger is not unlike the slightly larger Avelignese from the Italian side. However, it is a different breeds with distinct characteristics.

The Haflinger may have been the result of native stock breeding with Oriental horses which were left behind when the Ostrogoths were driven north by the Byzantine forces in the sixth century. Another story is that King Louis IV of

PAGES 108–111: Haflingers have many uses including light draft, harness work, and various under-saddle disciplines such as endurance riding and dressage.

Germany gave a Burgundian stallion to his son as a wedding gift, which was mated with local mares of Oriental origin to produce the Haflinger breed; either way there is little doubt that Oriental blood is present.

However, it is a definite fact that the modern Haflinger breed was improved in 1868 when the Arab stallion El Bedavi XXII was imported to the region and bred with Haflinger mares; today, all Haflingers are related to this one stallion.

The Arab blood can clearly be seen in the fine head which is in sharp contrast to the stocky body. Nowadays, the Haflinger is still to be found in Austria, where it is closely monitored in government-organized breeding programs as well as by private individuals. The breed is also popular the world over, particularly in Europe. It is useful in harness, and as a children's riding pony and family pet.

Appearance: The Haflinger has a noble Arab head with a slightly dished nose, large, attentive eyes, small alert ears, and neat nostrils and muzzle. The neck is well-proportioned with fine sloping shoulders, good withers and a deep girth. The body is broad and strong with muscular quarters and a high-set tail. The legs are of medium length with very strong, tough hooves.

Characteristics: The Haflinger is a sociable animal and enjoys the company of people. It is intelligent, trustworthy, and docile, making it an excellent work pony as well as children's pet. Haflingers are hardy and require only moderate feeding; however, they do require shelter from cold winds and wet weather. Their most striking feature is their flaxen mane and tail.

HANOVERIAN

Country of Origin: Germany

Colors: All solid colors

Height: 15.2–17 hh

The Hanoverian is one of the most important horse breeds in the world. Today, there are 16,000 registered brood mares and more than 400 stallions. The breed has a long history, the earliest reference to it being in the eighth century when it was used at the Battle of Poitiers, in which Charles Martel stemmed the advance of the Saracens. These were heavy warhorses, probably a mixture of native, Spanish, and Oriental influences.

The horses owe their evolution to warfare, and by the Middle Ages developed to be large, cob-like and capable of carrying a knight together with his heavy armor. The type was favored for many centuries, but changes in warfare techniques meant that a lighter horse was eventually required. At this time the Hanoverian was still a heavy breed, even though it was taller and more agile than the cob type; by the seventeenth century there were three distinctive types of horse bred for military purposes: the Hanoverian, Mecklenburg, and Danish.

In the eighteenth century, the Hanoverian truly came into its own, when a member of the House of Hanover in the person of George I ascended the British throne in 1714, but spent much of his reign in Hanover; for the next 100 years or so the Hanoverian was improved. English Thoroughbred stallions were bred with Hanoverian mares, and Cleveland Bay was also added to produce a horse that was still quite heavy and which was used for farm and coach work.

It was George II who established the state stud at Celle in 1735, where horses for agriculture, riding, and driving were bred. Here the Hanoverian breed was improved still further with the addition of Thoroughbred and Trakehner blood; the Hanoverian breed registry was founded in 1888. The end result was a horse which is similar to the fabulous competition horse of today—probably the best known of all warmbloods—which excels the world over in top dressage and show jumping. Nowadays, the Society of Breeders of the Hanoverian Warmblood Horse is responsible for the purity of the breed. Approximately 150–160, most of them stallions, are kept by the state and are based at Celle, where they are required to undergo tests for soundness,

conformation, and character for several months before they are allowed to mate. Hanoverians are often used to improve other warmblood breeds.

Hanoverians now come in two types: the heavier ones are used for show jumping, while the lighter ones, which have more Thoroughbred blood, are used for dressage.

Appearance: The Hanoverian is near-perfect in conformation and its Thoroughbred characteristics are immediately discernible. The head is of medium size with a straight nose and keen, alert eyes and pricked ears. The neck has a graceful arch and is long and muscular, while the chest is well-developed with a deep girth and sloping shoulder. The back is of medium length with muscular loins and powerful quarters. The legs are strong with large joints and the hooves are well-shaped.

Characteristics: The most important feature of the Hanoverian and one of the important tests that stallions have to undergo at Celle is one of character: only horses with an even temperament and a willing nature are allowed to breed. Hanoverians are noble and proud with an excellent free-flowing action which allows them to excel at advanced dressage.

The Hanoverian's Thoroughbred breeding is clearly evident in its fine features and noble countenance.

HOLSTEIN

Country of Origin: Germany

Colors: Most commonly bay, though all solid colors, together with gray, are permitted

Height: 16–17 hh

The Holstein or Holsteiner is thought to be the oldest of the warmblood breeds, tracing back more than 700 years. It is probably descended from a native breed called the Marsh Horse, which once roamed the wetlands of the Elbe estuary in what is now called Schleswig-Holstein. The first written records relating to the Holstein date back to the thirteenth century when Gerhard I, Count of Holstein and Storman, allowed the monks of the monastery at Uetersen grazing rights for the quality horses they bred. These were native stock mixed with Andalusian, Neapolitan, and Oriental blood to produce a heavy, useful horse which was valued by farmers for its strength and reliability and as a military horse for its courage, stamina, and ability. It also earned favor as a coach horse. After the Reformation, the monastery land was returned to the landowners who continued the horse-breeding tradition.

By 1686, the Holstein was so respected that strict guidelines were introduced to protect the breed which had by now become popular throughout Europe. By the eighteenth century, the Holstein's reputation was so great that vast numbers of horses were exported. Unfortunately, not all horses were bred to the exacting standards that had once prevailed and the breed began to deteriorate.

PAGES 114–117: The Holstein is greatly respected as a competition horse, excelling at dressage, show jumping, and eventing.

By the nineteenth century the decline was halted, and measures were taken to save and improve the breed. As the demand for warhorses grew less, the Holstein was needed as a quality carriage horse; for this purpose, Yorkshire Coach Horses and Cleveland Bay stallions were mated with Holstein mares, which was a great success, and the breed received a new lease on life.

After World War II, Thoroughbred was also added to refine the breed, which also improved the Holstein's jumping ability and general character. Today, it is a supreme sport horse which excels at showjumping, dressage, and eventing. However, it also makes a wonderful riding horse, but does require plenty of exercise. It has also been bred to good effect with other warmblood breeds, most effectively with the Hanoverian.

Appearance: The Holstein is quite different from other warmbloods in that it has a large, rangy build with a huge stride. The head is long and straight with large, flaring nostrils. The ears are expressive and the eyes are large and gentle. The long neck is elegant and well-developed, with high withers; the back is long and straight. The shoulders are shapely and sloping, contributing to the huge stride. The chest is broad and the girth is deep, while the quarters are slightly sloping, muscular, and powerful. The legs are long and muscular.

Characteristics: The Holstein is a beautiful, well-balanced horse with an amazing ground-covering, elastic stride. The overall effect is of a horse that is elegant and which carries itself lightly. It is good-natured, obedient and eager to work.

ICELANDIC

Country of Origin: Iceland

Colors: Solid colors including palomino, gray, and pinto

Height: 12–14.2 hh

The Icelandic is a unique breed of smallish horses that came to Iceland with the first settlers 1,100 years ago. The Icelandic is derived from the Fjord and Døle horses of Norway, and the Celtics, Shetlands, Highlands, and Connemaras of the British Isles, which were brought to Iceland by Celts and Vikings in the ninth century. Because of the limited space on board their ships, the cargo would have consisted of only the best specimens; once settled, the invaders allowed their horses to mate freely together to produce the Icelandic breed as we know it today. This resulted in a hardy animal which lived in a semi-wild condition and was able to survive Arctic winters. It was mainly used for farming and for riding over icy terrain.

It is interesting to note that in 982, the importation of horses was banned to prevent the spread of disease, as a result of which the Icelandic was allowed to interbreed; however, later selective breeding means that conformation and health faults have been all but eradicated.

Historically, the Icelanders have been protective of their breed, wishing to preserve it in the country where it evolved. Nowadays, however, they are exported to other countries where they are popular as children's riding ponies as well as for trekking. Even though the Icelandic is a pony in stature, it is always referred to as a horse.

Appearance: The Icelandic is well-constructed. The head is of medium length, having a typical pony character with

Icelandics are ideal for children, being hardy, agile, and with plenty of stamina.

small pricked ears and soft, expressive eyes. The neck is well-set, and the chest is broad with a deep girth. The body and legs are stocky and strong and the feet are extremely hard.

Characteristics: The Icelandic is ideal for children, being tough and hardy and happy to live out all year round. The pony has two extra gaits: the tölt, which is a running walk with four beats, and is as fast as a canter and very comfortable; and the flying pace, which makes great demands on horse and rider and which has two beats and is used for racing. The pony can reach speeds of up to thirty miles per hour (48 km/h) and is impressive to watch. However, it is late to mature and shouldn't be backed until the age of four.

Icelandics live to a ripe old age, often working up until they are thirty; in fact, an Icelandic in Britain is known to have died aged forty-two.

IRISH DRAFT

Country of Origin: Ireland

Colors: Bay, brown, chestnut, or gray

Height: 15–17 hh

The Irish Draft is the national horse breed of Ireland and is one of the most prized and widely distributed horses in the world. Its history can be traced back to the Celts who invaded Ireland and brought many breeds with them, most notably Oriental and Spanish horses which they mated with their Celtic Ponies. Later, in the Middle Ages, Ireland was settled by the Norman-English and their much larger, heavier horses would have been of European origin. These were bred with the Irish horse to produce a more substantial animal which was of use to farmers, being capable of plowing, hauling, general riding, as well as hunting over Ireland's often difficult terrain.

By the eighteenth century, the Irish Draft was improved with additions of Thoroughbred and Arab blood and possibly also Barb and Turkmene. The result is a horse of excellent conformation, still capable of heavy work, but one which excels as a riding horse. It had all the docility and common sense of a heavier, coldblooded breed, but with the sparkle and verve of a hotblooded Arab or Thoroughbred.

During the Potato Famine of 1845–46 the Irish Draft's numbers diminished; Ireland's economy was in a state of turmoil and horse breeding ceased. By the end of the century the breed had picked up, along with a change of attitude, when it was decided to introduce heavier stock, such as Clydesdale and Shire, to make it a much bigger, heavier draft horse. In 1917, a stud book was opened, but by the end of World War I the breed was once again in danger, as mechanized transport began to dominate farming and haulage. By now, the Irish Draft was predominantly a riding horse, particularly a hunter.

By the early twentieth century, however, more Thoroughbred blood was introduced to produce the horse we know today. The breed is still predominantly a hunter, but it has been mixed with other breeds, particularly the Thoroughbred, to make it a superb competition horse

The Irish Draft was bred as an all-rounder, equally capable of work around the farm as a day out hunting over difficult terrain.

which has inherited the Irish Draft's love of jumping, excelling at both cross-country and eventing. A little of the Irish Draft is also present in some steeplechasers.

Appearance: The head is neat, with a straight nose, medium-length ears, and a noble mien. The neck is shortish and very strong with slightly pronounced withers and a long sloping shoulder. The chest is broad and the girth is deep. The back is medium-length and well-muscled, with strong loins and sloping, powerful quarters. The legs are sturdy and muscular with good bone, and the hooves are large and round.

Characteristics: The Irish Draft has all the substance of a medium-weight draft horse, but its hotblood ancestry has also given it its refined appearance, with no excess hair on the legs as in most heavier breeds. It has great stamina, agility, and courage.

KABARDIN

Country of Origin: Russia

Colors: All solid colors, also gray and occasionally roan

Height: 15.1–16.1 hh

The Kabardin is a breed from the Caucasus, currently part of the Kabardino-Balkaria region of Russia. It is descended from the Tarpan—the wild horse of eastern Europe and western Asia, which sadly became extinct in captivity in 1887. The Kabardin remained unchanged in type until the Russian Revolution when, like many other Russian breeds, steps were taken to improve it. The original Kabardin was bred with Karabakh, Turkmene, Persian, and Arab blood to create a much bigger, stronger horse which could be used for riding and general farm work, also as a pack animal.

It is an excellent mountain horse, being sure-footed, agile, and intelligent, with the innate ability to search out the safest route. It has great stamina, enabling it to work all day under the harshest conditions without tiring.

The breed remains popular to this day in its place of origin, where it is still used for light draft work and for riding. Elsewhere, it is used as a competition horse and also to improve other breeds.

Appearance: The head is quite long, often with a slightly Roman nose. The longish ears point inwards and are set close together. The eyes are wise and intelligent and the nostrils flared. The neck is long and well-developed and the back is straight and strong; the legs are long and fine, but nevertheless very strong. The overall impression is of a horse with strong Oriental influences.

Characteristics: The Kabardin is a hardy breed capable of living out all year round, given extra feeding. It has a good constitution and mostly lives to a ripe old age. It is kind, obedient, trustworthy and intelligent.

The Kabardin is descended from the now-extinct Tarpan. It was infused with other breeds to produce a large, sturdy animal which is sure-footed and has great stamina.

KLADRUBER

Country of Origin: Czech Republic

Colors: Gray and black, or faded black

Height: 16.2–17 hh

The Kladruber is a rare breed of horse that originated in the Czech Republic and is the only indigenous horse breed of the country. The breed was established in 1597 by the Emperor Maximilian II of Austria, where it was bred at the Kladruber Stud which is situated in the former Czechoslovakia. Today, the stud still produces Kladruber horses, which are composed of many different breeds. Heavy Alpine mares were originally mated with Barb and Turkish stallions, then later with Andalusian, Neapolitan, and Lipizzaner, resulting in horses that were used exclusively to draw coaches and appear in parades of the Austrian Court in Vienna.

However, World War II eventually took its toll on the breed with numbers plummeting to dangerously low levels; it was therefore decided to revive and improve the breed by adding Anglo-Norman, Hanoverian, and Oldenburg blood, which was mixed with the remaining stock. Today, the Kladruber is doing well and is used for general riding and for light haulage.

Appearance: The Kladruber has inherited many of the attributes of the Andalusian, Neapolitan, and Lipizzaner. The head is noble with a broad forehead, straight or slightly Roman nose, medium well-shaped ears, and an alert expression with large, kind, and intelligent eyes. The neck is high-set and well-developed; the girth is deep and the chest broad. The body is of medium length and is sturdy with large quarters. The legs are well-muscled with good bone and well-shaped hooves.

Characteristics: The Kladruber has an equable temperament and is a willing and obedient worker. It has an attractive high-stepping action.

PAGES 124–127: The Kladruber is impressive and proud. It is an amalgam of many breeds, including Andalusian, Neapolitan, and Lipizzaner, to name but a few.

KNABSTRUP

Country of Origin: Denmark

Colors: There are various color permutations similar to the appaloosa, such as white with chestnut, bay, and black. One overall color or roan is also possible

Height: 15.2–15.3 hh

The Knabstrup or Knabstrupper breed was first established in 1812 in Denmark, but its ancestry is far more ancient. The Knabstrup exhibits the same color patterns as the appaloosa as they share the same color genes from prehistoric spotted ponies. The Knabstrup is unusual for a European horse in that it has a distinctive spotted coat.

In the sixteenth and seventeenth centuries, spotted horses were very popular at European courts, but the Knabstrup was founded much later, in the early 1800s, when an Iberian mare of the Knabstrup Estate in Denmark was mated with a palomino Frederiksborg stallion. The foal was born with a spotted coat of many colors which also had an attractive sheen. This became the foundation stallion of the Knabstrup breed.

Unfortunately, because subsequent horses were bred primarily for their unusual coats, insufficient care and attention was given to their conformation, leading to gradual deterioration, when the breed lost its popularity and almost disappeared. In recent years, the horse has been improved with the addition of Thoroughbred blood and is popular once again. Today, it is used as a general riding horse and also features in showing classes and, because of its spots, even the circus.

The Knabstrup's most distinctive feature is its spotted coat, which makes it popular as a circus performer. However, is it mainly used a a riding horse.

Appearance: The head is large with a straight or Roman nose. The ears are small and well-pricked and the eyes have a kind, gentle expression. The muzzle is square with large, open nostrils. The neck is high-set and there are well-developed shoulders and a broad chest. The back is rather long with slightly sloping quarters, and the legs are strong with good bone. The mane and tail are rather sparse.

Characteristics: The Knabstrup is a good-quality riding horse with excellent natural paces. It is kind and intelligent, easy to train, and an obedient and willing worker.

LATVIAN

Country of Origin: Latvia

Colors: All solid colors and gray

Height: 15.1–16 hh

The Latvian is a warmblood breed originating in Latvia. Breeding began in Latvia in the early twentieth century and so the breed has no ancient history, though no one can be certain of its origins; but the general opinion is that it is either descended from the prehistoric Forest Horse, a heavy type that once roamed over much of northern Europe, or that it evolved from an indigenous Lithuanian pony crossed with Tarpan and Arab blood. It is thought that the latter is more likely.

Today, there are three distinctive types of Latvian, depending on the other breeds with which it has become intermingled. The heaviest is the Latvian Draft which is the original breed present in the other two and which has been infused with Finnish Draft, Oldenburg, and Ardennes to make a substantial draft horse which is not so heavy that it cannot be ridden. The medium-sized version is the Latvian Harness Horse, which came into being in the 1920s when the original Latvian was bred with Hanoverian, Oldenburg, and Norfolk Roadster to make a lighter and more elegant carriage horse. The final, lighter, Latvian is a more recent addition, having received infusions of Arab and Thoroughbred to make a horse which is more of a warmblood and does well in competition. Today, all three are still used by farmers and competition riders.

Appearance: The three types may vary in stature, but they are all unmistakably Latvian. The head is longish and noble with a straight nose and large nostrils, proud eyes, and small well-shaped ears. The neck is long and nicely placed with sloping shoulders, a deep girth, and a longish body with well-developed quarters. The legs are shapely though volume of bone depends on type. The mane and tail are thick and full.

Characteristics: Latvians are incredibly strong with excellent stamina and an equable temperament.

PAGES 130–133: Latvians come in three distinctive types, the lightest is used as a competition horse.

LIPIZZANER

Country of Origin: Austria

Colors: The Lipizzaner is famous for its gray (white) coat. Foals are born dark, but most lighten to become pure white by the age of seven. Few remain brown or black

Height: 15–15.3 hh

The Lipizzaner is a breed of horse originating from Lipica in Slovenia. It is probably one of the world's most recognizable breeds due to its association with the Spanish Riding School of Vienna, where the horses are trained using traditional methods that date back hundreds of years, based on the principles of classical dressage. Despite its origins in what is now Slovenia, the Lipizzaner has a much more ancient history, dating back to the eighth century and the Moorish occupation of Spain. The Moors brought with them horses of Oriental origin, such as Arabs and Barbs. These were bred with the heavier Iberian horses, which in turn produced the Andalusian which is the most important element in the Lipizzaner's breeding.

PAGES 134–137: Only Lipizzaner stallions are used in Haute école in the Spanish Riding School.

In 1580, Archduke Charles, son of the Holy Roman Emperor Ferdinand I, and who had inherited Austria-Hungary, sought to improve his horses, deciding to school them in *haute école*, a form of equitation that featured spectacular leaps into the air, which was becoming increasingly popular. To this end, he founded a stud at Lipizza, which also specialized in breeding carriage horses, and filled it with quality Spanish (Iberian) horses, known to be capable of the discipline. He used these as the foundation stock of the Lipizzaner, crossing them with heavier native breeds as well as Barb, Arab, Andalusian, and other European breeds such as Neapolitan and Kladruber. Thus, over a period of several hundred years, the classical riding horse was born.

The Spanish Riding School of Vienna, that most famous riding establishment, had been founded in 1572. The name was not due to its Spanish riding traditions but because of the Spanish origins of the horses. The aim of the school was to teach the art of classical equestrianism to men of noble breeding. The original venue was a crude wooden structure which was replaced by the splendid building which was commissioned by Charles VI in 1735 and which is still in use today. The Spanish Riding School is stocked exclusively with Lipizzaner stallions.

When the Austrian-Hungarian Empire collapsed, the stud was moved to Piber in Austria, and during World War II was evacuated to Germany for its own protection. Today, the Lipizzaner is bred mainly at Piber (which supplies all the stallions for the Spanish Riding School) but also at Lipizza and Babolna in Hungary, and in the Czech Republic, Slovenia and Romania. Nowadays, as well as performing in the Spanish Riding School of Vienna, the Lipizzaner is also used as a draft horse and for carriage driving. They are also becoming popular as general riding horses.

Appearance: The Lipizzaner breed was based on six foundation stallions, and their different characteristics can be seen in its descendants today. Lipizzaners can therefore vary according to which of the six bloodlines has been used, but generally speaking they are of an Iberian type, similar to the Lusitano and Andalusian. The head is large with either a straight or Roman nose. The ears are finely pointed and alert and the eyes kind and intelligent. The neck is well-set, powerful, and well-muscled with a good crest. The chest is wide with a deep girth. The shoulders can be slightly straight and short. The back is long but strong and muscular with powerful quarters and a slightly low-set tail. The legs are shortish but powerful, with small, well-shaped, tough hooves.

Characteristics: The noble Lipizzaner possesses all the qualities of its breeding: the agility and balance of its Iberian forebears as well as the stamina and refinement of the Oriental. They combine stamina and endurance with natural balance and agility, are kind, intelligent, willing, and obedient, but with plenty of sparkle. They are late to mature, usually around the age of seven, and should not be worked too young. However, they stay sound for a long time and usually live to a good age.

LUSITANO

Country of Origin: Portugal

Colors: All solid colors as well as gray

Height: 15–16 hh

The Lusitano, also known as the Pure Blood Lusitano is a Portuguese horse breed. It shares its heritage with the Andalusian, both being descended from the Iberian riding horse. Until the 1960s, they were considered one breed, under the Andalusian name. The Lusitano gets its name, which was only adopted in the early twentieth century, from Lusitania, the Roman name for Portugal. The origins of the breed go back to around 25,000 BC to the ancient ancestors of the Sorraia breed which can be seen in cave paintings in the Iberian peninsula.

Unlike the Andalusian, the Lusitano's breeding has remained much truer to its Sorraia ancestry, with infusions limited to Oriental, Garrano, and Spanish blood. This mix hasn't changed for centuries and today, care is taken only to use horses with obvious Iberian characteristics to keep the breed true to type.

The Lusitano was mainly bred for and still is used for working the farms around the fertile River Tagus and also for bullfighting, known as the corrida, as well as for *haute école*. In Portugal the bull is thankfully not killed and the whole event is performed with the rider on horseback.

PAGES 138–143: The Lusitano has a shared heritage with the Andalusian of Spain, both being descended from Iberian stock.

Nevertheless the Lusitano has to be incredibly agile and fast to avoid injury.

These horses are highly prized and receive *haute école* schooling to enhance their precision so that they can survive the demanding and dangerous spectacle. The Lusitano stallions are trained to these high standards before they are sent to stud, and all fighting horses are left entire; it is thought that geldings lack the courage and intelligence to work in the bullring.

Today they are still used for farm work, bullfighting, and also for lower levels of dressage. Infusions of Lusitano are also used to improve other breeds.

Appearance: The Lusitano has a noble countenance. The head is quite long with a straight or slightly Roman nose and flared nostrils. The ears are of medium length, well-shaped, and alert. The eyes are keen and intelligent, the neck is set high with a well-developed muscular crest and well-defined withers. The sloping shoulders are powerful and the chest is broad with a deep girth. The back is short and strong and the loins broad, with quarters that are not too large. The Lusitano's high-stepping action is attributed to its strong, long hocks which are capable of great impulsion with deep flexion achieved by a well-developed second thigh (stifle).

Characteristics: This noble and courageous horse is kind, good-natured, and obedient. It is level-headed and not given to panic, important attributes in a fighting horse.

MANGALARGA MARCHADOR

Country of Origin: Brazil

Colors: All solid colors, roan, and pinto

Height: Usually around 15 hh

The Mangalarga Marchador is a horse breed native to Brazil of which there are over 350,000 registered both in Brazil and abroad. For centuries, Brazil and Portugal were closely connected and at one time were under the same ruler, Don Joao VI, in around 1815. It was he who brought quality Portuguese and Spanish horses to Brazil, particularly the Altér Real and Andalusian.

The Mangalarga is a direct descendant of one particular Altér Real stallion which was mated with Criollo mares; later, more Altér Real, Barb, and Andalusian were added to improve the breed. The result is neat, lightly-built, and strongly reminiscent of the Barb, but with the rolling gait of the Spanish breeds.

It is most often used for riding the enormous *estancias* of Brazil, where its fifth gait, known as the *marcha*, makes it fast but comfortable for the rider. The *marcha* is a cross between a trot and a canter, which the horse can maintain for great distances. The horse's name is a combination of the words Mangalarga, from the name of the *hacienda*, and *marcha*. Today, the Mangalarga Marchador is also used for endurance and trail riding, jumping, and polo. It is an excellent all-round riding and showing horse.

Appearance: The head is high and proud with medium-length ears and intelligent eyes. The nose is straight with flaring nostrils. The back is long with strong loins and neat quarters; the shoulders are sloping with a deep girth and there are well-muscled legs with hard hooves.

Characteristic:s The Mangalarga has incredible stamina which enables it to work all day and cover huge distances. It is good-natured, willing, and obedient.

Mangalarga Marchadors are neat and lightly built, reminiscent of the Barb, but with a rolling gait.

MARWARI

Country of Origin: India

Colors: All colors, including roan and pinto

Height: 15.3–16.1 hh

The Marwari is rare breed of horse from the Marwar region of Rajasthan in India. It is famous for its inward-turning ear tips. The breed has featured in Indian art over the centuries.

The Marwari is unusual in that it has a fifth gait, called the *revaal*, which is a long, smooth action with little vertical movement and very comfortable for the rider. Marwari numbers declined during the British occupancy of India, but thanks to today's Rajput families and others interested in the continuation of the breed, the Marwari is once again flourishing. It is now used as a dancing horse, popular at weddings and festivals. The dance is a form of *haute école*, which the horse would have been taught when it was a warhorse long ago.

Appearance: The Marwari has a high, proud head-carriage with a straight or slightly Roman nose, its trademark ears curving inward until they almost join together in the center. The eyes are large, bright, and intelligent; the neck is of medium length and arches in movement. The coat is fine and silky.

Characteristics: The Marwari has a naturally flamboyant presence and the will to perform. However, it is also tough and is able to survive harsh conditions. It is courageous, intelligent, and a willing worker.

PAGES 146–149: The Marwari was once a great warhorse and featured in Indian art for centuries. Thanks to renewed interest, the breed is once again gaining in popularity.

MISSOURI FOX TROTTER

Country of Origin: U.S.A.

Colors: All solid colors, including pinto

Height: 14–16.1 hh

The Missouri Fox Trotter is a breed from the state of Missouri in the United States. It was developed in the nineteenth century by settlers in Missouri and Arkansas. Initially, its purpose was to be a general riding horse with the speed and endurance to cope with difficult terrain. The foundation stock for the breed was the Morgan, which was infused with Thoroughbred and Arab as well as Iberian blood. As horses with elaborate gaits became more popular, the breed was later mated with Saddlebred and Tennessee Walking Horse which greatly improved its elegance, bearing, and paces, including its foxtrot gait; this is basically a diagonal gait like the trot, in which the horse appears to walk with the front legs while trotting with the hind.

In the early days, before racing was made illegal, the Fox Trotter had been a useful competitor, but after the ban it was once again used as a general riding horse.

A stud book for the breed was eventually opened in 1948. The breed society, however, placed strict guidelines that the Missouri Fox Trotter should have no artificial aids to influence and enhance its gait, such as nicking or setting the tail; consequently, its action is not as pronounced or extravagant as, for example, the American Saddlebred. The breed is popular in the United States, where it is used for general riding, showing, and endurance.

Appearance: The head is a little plain, with a straight nose and a square muzzle with large open nostrils. The ears are medium-length and alert and the eyes have a kind but intelligent expression. The neck is medium-length and fairly well-developed with prominent withers; the back is short, with strong loins and hindquarters. The tail is set fairly low; the legs are long with large joints and well-shaped, strong hooves.

Characteristics: The Missouri Fox Trotter has a charming, easy-going nature. It is willing and obedient with excellent stamina.

Unlike the Saddlebred, the breed standard for the Fox Trotter bans any artificial aid to improve its natural paces.

MORGAN

Country of Origin: U.S.A.

Colors: All solid colors are acceptable

Height: 14–15.2 hh

The Morgan horse is one of the earliest horse breeds developed in the United States. It is America's most famous and versatile breed. All Morgans can be traced back to just one stallion called Figure, later renamed Justin Morgan after its owner, Thomas Justin Morgan, a tavern keeper and singing teacher who supplemented his income by breeding stallions.

The colt was born in around 1790 in Vermont. It is thought that its sire was called True Briton, probably a Welsh Cob, but little is known concerning the dam; however, it is thought that she had some Oriental and Thoroughbred blood.

Thomas Justin Morgan was so impressed with Figure's looks and personality that he eventually decided to put him to stud. The results were remarkable: it did not matter what mare Justin Morgan covered, a foal the image of its father was produced. Moreover, the performance of each one was second to none, the sire's prowess as a marvelous harness and riding horse having been replicated in its offspring. In fact, it is quite amazing that such a significant and impressive breed developed from just one stallion.

Today, Morgans are just as versatile–used in harness competitions, shows, driving, trail riding, and driving.

Appearance: The head should give immediate evidence of quality, with beautiful and expressive eyes. The muzzle is small and the profile straight or slightly dished. The neck is well-crested and the shoulders strong. The hindquarters are large and strong and the legs sturdy.

Some Morgans are bred particularly for their high-stepping action, a type known as the Park Morgan. The other type is the Pleasure Morgan, whose action is less exaggerated.

Characteristics: Morgans are strong, versatile, hard-working, and have a spirited but tractable nature.

PAGES 152–155: The elegant Morgan is a truly remarkable breed in that it originated from just one stallion.

NEW FOREST

Country of Origin: U.K.

Colors: All solid colors are acceptable

Height: 12–14.2 hh

The New Forest pony is indigenous to the New Forest in Hampshire in southern England, where equines have lived since before the last Ice Age. It is likely that the breed is a descendant of the Celtic Pony, as are all the British native breeds, though the earliest mention of it dates to the time of King Canute (ca. 995–1035), who famously sought to stop the sea's rising tide.

The New Forest consists mainly of scrubland, bog, and moorland, which has led to the development of a hardy animal designed to survive harsh conditions. Over the years, Thoroughbred and Arab blood were introduced, mainly to increase size and performance and to improve the pony's appearance, but is was not until the end of the nineteenth century, during the reign of Queen Victoria, that a structured breeding program was initiated. At the same time, other British breeds were also introduced, such as the Dartmoor, Exmoor, Welsh, Fell, Dales, and Highland.

In 1891, the Society for the Improvement of New Forest Ponies was founded to ensure that there was an ample supply of quality stallions living in the New Forest and this in turn led to the official publication of the first stud book in 1910. Nowadays, although still living and breeding in their home environment, many quality New Forest Ponies are also bred in private studs all over the world.

Appearance: This is one of the larger breeds native to Britain. It is an ideal child or teenager's pony and excellent for driving. It has a well-proportioned body that is more slender than other British breeds, and well-formed feet.

Characteristics: New Forests have a lovely temperament. They are calm, good-natured, and a pleasure to own. They are used for dressage, show jumping, and cross-country. In fact, a good New Forest Pony can rise to any occasion.

PAGES 156–159: New Forest ponies are plentiful and can easily be seen when visiting the New Forest in Hampshire, England.

NORTH SWEDISH

Country of Origin: Sweden

Colors: All the usual solid colors, also roan

Height: 15–15.2 hh

The North Swedish is a breed of small heavy horse. It was traditionally used for forestry and agricultural work. This is another breed that can trace is origins back to the prehistoric Celtic Pony. It shares much of its ancestry with the Norwegian Døle, and has Friesian, Norfolk Trotter, Heavy Draft, and Thoroughbred in its make-up.

The breed has split into two distinctive types: the lighter version known as the North Swedish Trotter, which is capable of covering 0.62 mile (1km) in 1 minute 30 seconds, and which is faster than many other breeds recognized for speed. The heavier draft type is of greater stature and is used for general farm and haulage work.

Appearance: Like the Døle, the breed resembles a large pony. The head is small and neat with a broad forehead, straight or slightly Roman nose, and a squarish muzzle. The ears are small and alert and the eyes kind and inquisitive. The neck is short and well-developed with a slight crest. The chest and shoulders are powerful, the girth is deep, and the back is long with well-muscled hindquarters. The legs are rather short but sturdy, with good bone, hard hooves, and feathering around the heels. The heavy type has rather more bone and substance.

Characteristic:s The North Swedish is tough, hardy and can expect a long life. It requires little care and feeding and has great stamina and endurance. It has a well-balanced, springy action; the trotting type has a particularly good turn of speed.

The North Swedish looks similar to an overgrown pony, and like most ponies, requires little care or extra feeding. It is full of character and has plenty of stamina.

OLDENBURG

Country of Origin: Germany

Colors: Black, brown, bay, chestnut, or gray

Height: 16.2–17.2 hh

This is one of the largest of the modern German warmbloods, originally bred as a carriage horse. It dates back to the early part of the seventeenth century when keen horse-breeder Count Anton Guenther of Oldenburg, in northwestern Germany, began the first breeding program.

The Oldenburg's earliest ancestor were heavy Friesian horses infused with Spanish and Arabian blood. The breed was stabilized in the nineteenth century by the introduction of Thoroughbred, Cleveland Bay, Yorkshire Coach Horse, Anglo-Norman, and Hanoverian stallions.

Though originally bred as carriage horses, the Oldenburg was also used by the military as a strong artillery horse. However, as the years passed, the need for such horses diminished and a demand for lighter riding horses for competition and pleasure arose. In the second half of the twentieth century, lighter breeds were again introduced, such as Thoroughbred, Trakehner, Hanoverian, and Westphalian. Nowadays, the modern-day Oldenburg excels at dressage and show jumping while retaining its ability as a carriage horse, still used for the purpose today.

Appearance: The Oldenburg is distinguished by its noble head and a proud, workmanlike air. It has a high-set neck, long shoulder, strong back, and a well-muscled croup with strong joints. With its large frame and long, active stride, it makes a elegant dressage horse or a powerful show jumper.

Characteristics: The Oldenburg could be said to resemble a hunter type. Its character is equable, making it a pleasant horse to handle and own.

PAGES 162–165: The Oldenburg has a varied pedigree based on Friesian, Spanish, and Arabian blood and later refined with Thoroughbred, Cleveland Bay, Yorkshire Coach Horse, Anglo-Norman, and Hanoverian.

ORLOV TROTTER

Country of Origin: Russia

Colors: Usually gray, black, or bay

Height: 15.2–17 hh

The Orlov, or Orloff, Trotter is one of the foremost breeds of its type in the world and the most famous breed in Russia, renowned for its outstanding trot, speed, and stamina. It was founded in the eighteenth century by Count Alexey Orlov, whose ambition was to produce a superb trotting horse, and to this end founded a stud at Ostrov, near Moscow. He brought in a large number of Arabians, among them two distinctive stallions—the beautiful, silvery-gray Smetanka, and the brown Sultan I. After one season, Orlov was left with a few progeny from Dutch Harddraver, Mecklenburg, Danish, Thoroughbred, and Arabian mares.

Orlov was not happy with his stud and wanted somewhere better with more grazing, which he found in Khrenovoye in the Voronezh region to the south of Moscow, a place he considered perfect for his purpose, with vast areas of grassland, clear, natural springs, and a dry climate.

The Khrenovoye Stud was thus founded in 1778, and the following year produced a colt called Polkan I, which in turn was mated with a Danish mare carrying Spanish blood. The result was a foal called Bars I, which eventually showed exceptional stamina and trotting abilities and became the foundation stallion of the Orlov breed.

The Orlov is famous for its exceptional action. Its quality ensured that it reigned supreme on the racetrack until the end of the nineteenth century, when newer breeds were introduced to the Russian racing scene. Unfortunately, the Orlov is now in crisis, due largely to the introduction of these faster breeds.

Appearance: The Orlov has a small, elegant head with a noble profile. The hindquarters are powerful and, like many trotters, the shoulders are straight.

Characteristics: Energetic, sure-footed and bold. Owing to its swift, balanced trot it is suitable for riding and driving as well as trotting.

PAGES 166–169: The Orlov Trotter is famous above all for its impressive action.

PASO FINO

Country of Origin: Puerto Rico

Colors: All colors

Height: 14–15 hh

The foundation of the smooth-gaited Paso Fino is old Spanish or Iberian stock. They have the same bloodlines, inherited from horses brought to the Americas by the Spanish *conquistadors* in the sixteenth century; however, different environments have caused slight variations in their evolution in terms of character and conformation.

The Paso Fino is a naturally gaited horse, like the Peruvian Paso or Stepping Horse and another lesser known breed from Colombia, and although it is predominantly a working horse on the coffee plantations of Puerto Rico, these gaits make it remarkable. They are spectacular to watch, the main ones being the *fino*, the classic gait of the show ring, performed with the horse balanced and collected, the *corto*, executed with only medium collection and light contact on the bit, and the *largo*, the speed form of the gait.

There are another two variants, the *sobre paso*, a much more natural gait in which the horse is allowed a loose rein and is relaxed, and which is used in general riding rather than the

The Paso Fino is famously known for its spectacular gaits—the fino, corto, *and* largo.

show ring; the other is the *andadura* which is a fast pacing gait. However, this is uncomfortable and is only performed for short periods. The rest of the time the horse's effortless gait makes it extremely comfortable and smooth to ride, its gliding action making it popular for trail riding. Paso Finos are also in great demand for showing and displays.

Appearance: The head is fine, almost Arab-like, with a straight nose and flaring nostrils, longish well-shaped ears, and intelligent eyes. The body is very Spanish, similar to the

Andalusian's, with a good sloping shoulder, well-developed neck, and medium-length back with slightly sloping quarters and a low-set tail. The legs are sturdy and strong with large hocks.

Characteristics: The Paso Fino has an excellent temperament. It has great enthusiasm and is obedient and easy to ride, seemingly enjoying the company of human beings. Despite its small stature it is very strong; in fact, even the smallest will easily carry a man over hills and rough terrain.

PERCHERON

Country of Origin: France

Colors: Mainly gray but occasionally black and dark chestnut.

Height: Small Percheron 14.1–16.1 hh
Large Percheron 16.1–17.3 hh

PAGES 172–175: There are two types of Percheron. The light version is used as a riding horse, while the heavier counterpart is still used on farms and for forestry work.

The Percheron originated in the Huisne River valley area, in the province of La Perche in Normandy, northern France. Originally bred as warhorses, but over time they began to be used for agriculture and hauling heavy goods. The breed is an ancient one dating back to 732, when Arab horses abandoned by the Saracens after their defeat at the Battle of Poitiers were allowed to breed with the local heavy mares of the region. From these matings the Percheron type emerged.

At this time the horse was much lighter than its modern counterpart and was used for riding as well as for light draft work. The type remained popular until the Middle Ages and the Crusades, when Arab and Barb horses from the Holy Land were mated with Percherons. It was also around this time that the Comte de Perche brought back Spanish horses from

his forays in Spain; these were also mated with the Percheron, with further infusions of Andalusian added later. By the eighteenth century, the original breed had become almost completely eradicated by the addition of Thoroughbred and more Arab; in 1820 two gray Arab stallions were mated with Percheron mares, which is responsible for the predominantly gray color of the modern-day breed.

By now, all the heaviness of the ancient breed had disappeared; consequently, heavy mares from other regions were bred with Percheron stallions to make them more suitable for agriculture and to formulate the breed as it is known today. The lighter Percheron still exists and is used as a heavy riding horse, while the heavy version is still used for farm and forestry work and, in some countries, for pulling drays. It is also popular in the show ring.

Over the years the Percheron has been heavily exported to other countries such as the United Kingdom, Canada, Australia, and other parts of Europe, which has helped its recognition as one of the world's leading heavy breeds.

Appearance: For a heavy breed the Percheron's head is proud and elegant, with a straight nose, broad forehead, expressive eyes, and short shapely ears. The neck is short to medium, well-developed, and with great strength. The shoulders are nicely sloping and well-shaped, with a broad chest and a deep girth. The Percheron is fairly short in the back, which adds to its strength, with slightly sloping but broad quarters. The legs are short and sturdy with well-shaped tough hooves with very little feather.

Characteristics: The Percheron possesses a good deal of elegance due to large amounts of Arab blood which have been added over the centuries. It has an excellent temperament, is calm, obedient, and easy to handle, and has a keen intelligence. It has a smooth but lively action, making it comfortable to ride.

PINTO HORSE

Country of Origin: U.S.A.

Colors: The Pinto is well-known for its striking coat, which can be black, chestnut, brown, bay, dun, sorrel, palomino, gray, or roan, patched with large areas of white. There are three distinctive types of coat pattern.

Tobiano, in which the head is like that of any solid-colored horse, but there are round or oval spots resembling shields running over the neck and chest. One or both flanks may be colored white or a color can predominate. The tail is often composed of two colors.

Overo, which is predominantly dark or white, though the white shouldn't cross the back between withers and tail. The head should be white with scattered irregular markings on the rest of the body. At least one leg should be dark and the tail is usually one color.

Tovero, which is a mixture of the two.

Height: 14.2–15.2 hh

PAGES 176–179: The Pinto or Paint Horse came about when Iberian horses which were brought over by the Spanish turned wild. Their coats are always white with colored patterning.

The Pinto or Paint Horse (from the Spanish *pintado*, meaning "painted"), like many of the old American breeds, is descended from Iberian horses that came over from Spain with the *conquistadors*. Depending on the country where are bred, they are sometimes called particolored, pied, piebald, calico, and skewbald, terms sometimes used to describe variations in color and markings.

In the United States, the Paint Horse is regarded as a separate breed. The American Paint Horse Association, formed in 1965 is concerned only with stock- and quarter-type horses.

The original Spanish horses were allowed to revert to a feral condition and gradually extended into North America, where they roamed the Western deserts. Once domesticated by Native Americans, however, they were greatly revered; in fact, the Pinto was believed to possess magic powers.

Ranchers also adopted these hardy horses, as their stamina and agility made them excellent for work over extensive distances. Today they are still used as workhorses but also at rodeos, and for trail riding and showing and as all-round riding horses.

Appearance: The Pinto has a fine head and graceful well-defined neck. The ears are alert and of medium length, while the eyes indicate spirit and intelligence. They are usually quite short in the back, with long, strong legs, and hard tough hooves.

Characteristics: Hardy and agile.

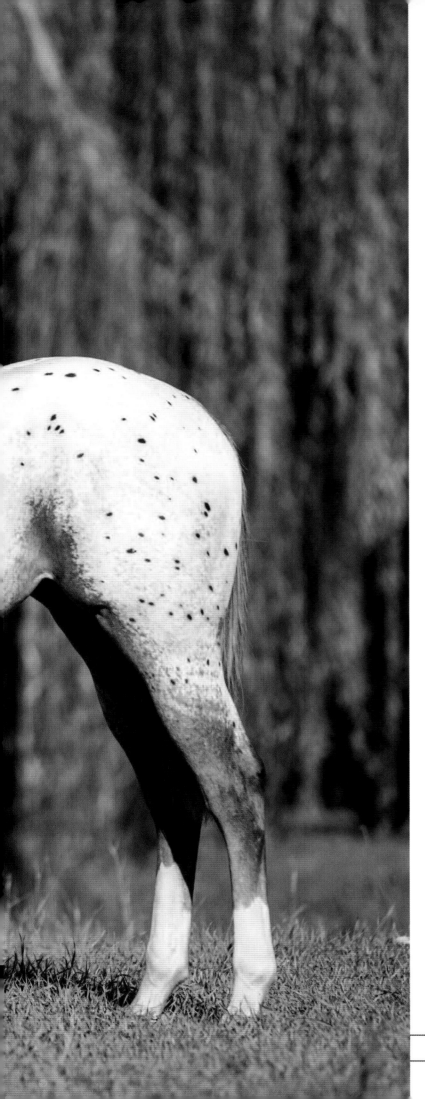

PONY OF THE AMERICAS

Country of Origin: U.S.A.

Colors: Similar to the Appaloosa

Height: 11.2–14 hh

The Pony of the Americas is a pony breed developed in the state of Iowa. This is a relatively new breed dating to the 1950s and is the result of an accidental crossing between a Scottish Shetland Pony and an Appaloosa mare with Iberian origins. The resulting offspring, Black Hand I, was a smaller version of its dam and it was this stallion that became the foundation of America's first pony breed. The breed registry was founded in 1954 and in just a short period of time had thousands of ponies registered with it.

The breed has the appearance of a small horse rather than a pony, and a little later was further refined with Quarter Horse and Arab blood to produce the showy, high-stepping action popular in the show ring.

Similar in stature to British Thoroughbred ponies, the Pony of the Americas is most popular with children, who find it easy to handle. It is also strong enough to carry a small adult and is used in endurance, trail riding, and show jumping as well as trotting and pony flat racing.

Appearance: The head is very Arab with a broad forehead, small pricked ears, and a straight or slightly dished nose. The eyes are large and kind. The body is of medium length with a good sloping shoulder, well-developed quarters, and fine but strong legs.

Characteristics: The Pony of the Americas is strong and hardy with a calm but willing disposition.

The Pony of the Americas is quite refined and similar in conformation to the British Thoroughbred pony. It has a high-stepping, attractive action.

POTTOK

Countries of Origin: France and Spain

Colors: All solid colors and pinto

Height: 12–13 hh

The Pottok is an endangered breed of pony native to the Pyrenees of France and Spain. Pottok means "a prehistoric animal hunted by cavemen." It is an ancient breed with mysterious origins, but it has always inhabited the west of the Basque region as well as Navarra, in Spain, and southwest France, where it remained a pure breed until the eighth century when it was bred with Arabs. Pottoks have been used on farms and as pit ponies in the mines of northern France.

The Basques have a great affection for the pony and it remains an important part of their culture. Many still live in a semi-wild state and some are used as general riding ponies. They are excellent jumpers, and are also used for trail riding, where their sure-footedness and familiarity with the terrain are great assets.

Appearance: The head is small and neat with a straight or slightly Roman nose. In winter the Pottok grows a moustache to protect the nose when foraging for food among cold, sparse vegetation. The neck is short and strong with a thick shaggy mane; the chest is broad, and the loins are long with slightly sloping hindquarters. The tail is low-set and very thick. The legs are strong with well-shaped hard hooves.

Characteristics: Pottoks have lively temperaments and are willing workers. They are good-natured, strong, and hardy.

The Pottok is from the Basque region of France and Spain, where it lives in a semi-wild state.

SELLE FRANÇAIS

Country of Origin: France

Colors: Mainly chestnut, although other colors are acceptable

Height: 15–17 hh

The Selle Français is a breed of sport horse from France. Many of the best-known breeds are a fusion of several others and the Selle Français is no exception. Breeders of this beautiful warmblood had been working for many years in their quest for the ultimate competition horse, and used a variety of breeds to achieve their goal. Finally, in the 1950s, the breed was given official status and was named the Selle Français or French Saddle Horse.

Its main ancestor is the Norman, dating back to the Middle Ages, itself a cross between indigenous mares and imported horses such as Arabs and other Orientals. The Norman's primary use was as a warhorse, but the line had also been influenced by German and Danish cart horses, along with Thoroughbred and Norfolk Roadster. Other infusions such as Limousin, Charentais, and Vendéen have also played their part in the breed's development.

The Selle Français is a combination of many breeds, from the heavy Norman to the English Thoroughbred, which was used to improve the breed and to produce a top-flight competition horse.

However, it was mainly Thoroughbred which was responsible for the athletic horse we know today. The breed excels as a competition horse and is particularly talented at show jumping, though it is a good eventer and hunter.

Appearance: The Selle Français is an elegant horse. The standard demands a fine head, sloping shoulders, and well-sprung ribs. The legs should be strong and the hindquarters powerful. There are up to five weights to suit individual tastes.

Characteristics: Like many of the warmblood breeds, the Selle Français has an even, placid temperament, but is also intelligent, willing, and energetic enough for top competition. The breed is reputed to be very quick to learn.

SHAGYA ARABIAN

Country of Origin: Hungary

Colors: All solid colors, though many inherit the Shagya stallion's gray color. Rarest of all is black

Height: 14.2–15.2 hh

The Shagya Arabian is a rare Arabian breed which is not very well-known worldwide. It comes from Hungary's second most famous breeding establishment, the Babolna Stud, founded in the late 1700s; the other one is Mezöhegyes.

In 1816, the military stipulated that all brood mares should be bred with Oriental stallions to provide cavalry and harness horses; stallions with mixed Oriental blood as well as Iberian crosses were also used. The results, although fairly lightweight, were horses that were tough and with plenty of stamina.

Following this success, it was decided that the Bobolna Stud should concentrate on breeding horses with predominantly Arab blood, which was the beginning of the excellent Shagya Arabian.

Today's breed is descended from one Arab stallion, called Shagya, which was brought from Syria in 1836. He was fairly large for an Arab, standing at 15.2$^{1}/_{2}$ hh, and was from the Siglavi or Seglawy strain. The stallion was typically Arab in conformation with a fine dished nose, a proud high-crested neck, short body, and high-set tail. It was mated with the military-style mares to produce the first Shagya Arabians and subsequent breeding by selection has produced a beautiful, refined riding horse of the highest quality. Today, Shagya Arabians make excellent riding and competition horses.

Appearance: The Shagya is very like the Arab in conformation, but a little heavier. The head is wedge-shaped with a wide forehead and a straight or dished nose. The ears are neatly pointed and alert and the eyes kind. The muzzle is small and delicate with large flaring nostrils. The neck is beautifully arched, well-muscled, and set high. The shoulders are sloping, with a broad chest and deep girth; the body is fairly short with well-defined quarters and long, elegant legs which are well-muscled at the top with more bone than the traditional Arab.

Characteristics: The Shagya has the constitution of the Arab but is bigger and stronger. It is kind, noble and spirited, with great stamina, speed and agility.

PAGES 192–195: Shagya Arabians stem from one stallion which came from Syria.

SHETLAND

Country of Origin: U.K.

Colors: Black, brown, bay, chestnut, gray, and pinto

Height: Up to a maximum height of 42 inches (107cm)

The Shetland pony is a distinctive British breed of pony originating in the Shetland Isles of Scotland. The islands lie off the coast in the far north of Scotland. The islands are remote and have a harsh climate, particularly in winter. There is not much shelter for the ponies and food is scarce, but they have adapted admirably to survive on very little and next to nothing during the winter months when they are known to come down from the hills and feed on seaweed that has been washed up on the beach.

It is unclear where the ponies originally came from, but there is evidence that they have been on the islands for a very long time, since Bronze Age remains were found dating from 2,500 years ago. Alternatively, they may have come from Scandinavia across the ice, or even from Europe.

Traditionally, Shetlands were used by islanders as riding, plowing, pack, and harness ponies. In 1870, the Londonderry Stud at Bressay, Scotland, fixed the type and character of the breed and, although no longer in existence, all today's best stock can be traced back to the famous Londonderry sires.

Appearance: The head is small and neat and can be slightly dished. The ears are small and the eyes open and bold. The neck, shoulders, and withers are well-defined; the chest and quarters must be strong and muscular. The mane and tail is profuse, with straight feathering on the legs. The coat is double-layered, a feature unique to the Shetland.

Characteristics: The Shetland has plenty of character and can be willful. Because it is relatively strong for its size, it may be too much for a small child, unless it has been properly trained and has good manners. However, when kept in a suitable environment, with adult help on hand, they make superb children's ponies.

PAGES 196–199: Shetland ponies have been living on Shetland for at least 2,500 years.

SHIRE

Country of Origin: U.K.

Colors: Bay, black, brown, and gray are the recognized colors of the breed. White feathers on the legs are preferred for the show ring and white face markings are common

Height: 16.2–18 hh

The Shire is a British breed of draft horse and is one of the most famous and distinctive of all horses. Furthermore, it is one of the largest and most majestic breeds in the world. Descended from medieval warhorses, whose immense strength enabled them to carry knights into battle wearing full armor, it was probably based on the Friesian with later infusions of Brabant. It was brought to England by the Dutch to drain the fens of East Anglia. However, it was not until the late nineteenth century that the best heavy horses in England were selected to develop the breed as it is known today.

The Shire's strength also made it suitable for agriculture and heavy haulage work, so initially the breed was established in Lincolnshire and Cambridgeshire where strong horses were required to cope with heavy fenland soil; but the Shire soon became widespread in Staffordshire, Leicestershire, and Derbyshire until it eventually spread over the whole of England.

PAGES 200–205: The Shire is the largest and strongest horse in the world, and as a heavy horse it also the most elegant and majestic.

Up until the 1930s, the Shire was widely seen across the country, but as farms began to make use of tractors the numbers dropped dramatically until the breed was in danger of disappearing altogether. Fortunately, the problem was realized by a few dedicated breeders who helped to promote the breed and restore its popularity.

The Shire Horse Society has worked tirelessly to raise funds and to encourage the spread of the breed to other countries. Today, there are active Shire Horse societies across Europe, the United States, Canada, and Australia. Although a few Shires are still used on farms today, it is mainly for the sheer pleasure of working them in their traditional roles. They are also used in plowing competitions, again, for pleasure, and for the same reason breweries use them in pairs to deliver beer locally, using normal mechanized transport for longer distances; the spectacle of these beautiful horses is obviously excellent publicity.

Appearance: The Shire's most significant feature is its sheer size and massive muscular conformation. It is the largest and strongest horse in the world and when mature weighs a ton or more. Built ultimately for strength, the chest is wide, the back short-coupled, the loins and quarters massive. The legs, joints and feet are sufficiently large to balance and support the Shire's size; the lower legs are covered with long, straight, silky feathers. In the show ring, white feathers are generally preferred as they help to accentuate the horse's action. Even though the Shire is such a large horse, it is not an ungainly heavyweight; in fact it is very much in proportion and quite beautiful to behold. The head is always noble and the nose slightly Roman. The eyes are large and wise.

Characteristics: The Shire is well-known for its patient, gentle and placid nature; it is a true "gentle giant." In fact, it is quite amazing that such a strong animal that weighs so much can be so easily handled and it is not uncommon to see them ridden or handled by children or small women. Their kindness is legendary.

STANDARDBRED

Country of Origin: U.S.A.

Colors: All solid colors, but mainly bay, black, brown, and chestnut

Height: 14.2–17.2 hh

Developed in North America, the Standardbred is recognized and admired all over the globe. It is famous for its trotting and pacing abilities and is widely used in harness racing throughout the world. The breed dates back 200 years when trotting races became sufficiently popular to warrant a breeding program for the purpose.

The founding sire of today's Standardbred was Messenger, a gray Thoroughbred, born in 1780 and imported to Philadelphia in 1788. While Messenger was bred for racing at a gallop, his own sire, Mambrino, had been responsible for a long dynasty of famous trotting coachhorses in England.

Messenger worked at stud for about 20 years and became famous for producing strong, talented trotters. Meanwhile, during the mid-1800s in New England, the Morgan breed was being used to produce a line of smaller trotters with a straight up-and-down action. The high-stepping action of the Morgan line was then combined with the long-reaching stride of the Messenger line and this increased the performance of the Standardbred no end.

The trot of a Standardbred appears huge in comparison to that of ordinary breeds and is a gait whereby the legs are moved in diagonal pairs. However, the "pace" is peculiar to this breed and is a gait where the horse moves its legs in lateral pairs. While the trot is natural to all horses, the pace generally has to be taught, although some Standardbreds will offer to pace from birth. Pacing is quicker than trotting as it allows the stride to be longer and more economical.

The term Standardbred was introduced in 1879 and derives from the time standard which was set to test the ability of harness racers. The Standardbred horse is required to cover a mile (0.6 km) in 2 minutes and 30 seconds. Since this first standard was set, improved breeding has enabled the modern Standardbred to beat this target easily.

The Standardbred is probably the most successful trotter, used in trotting races all over the world for the past 200 years.

Appearance: The head is in proportion to the horse's body and the eyes kind; the ears are indicative of alertness. The horse is muscular overall with a well-sprung barrel, sloping shoulder, and a strong back. The legs resemble those of the Thoroughbred, though are somewhat larger, with large joints; the hooves are large and strong.

Characteristics The Standardbred has an excellent temperament and away from the racetrack is quite placid. However, when racing it is highly competitive, and displays great stamina and unbounding energy. The Standardbred is considered people-oriented and easy-to-train.

Nowadays, Suffolks are shown, used in plowing competitions, or are owned by breweries.

Appearance: The Suffolk Punch is always chestnut in color (the traditional spelling for this particular breed is chesnut, without the "t"). The breed is well-known for its great strength and has an extremely powerful, muscular body with relatively short legs providing a low center of gravity, which in turn helps the horse to pull plows or vehicles more easily.

Characteristics: The Suffolk is well-known for being easy to train, docile, and hardworking.

SWEDISH WARMBLOOD

Country of Origin: Sweden

Colors: All solid colors

Height: 16.1–17 hh

The Swedish Warmblood is one of the oldest breeds of Warmblood breeds. Like many European warmbloods it was developed to produce a supreme cavalry horse, with strength, stamina, intelligence, and courage.

In the seventeenth century, the Royal Stud at Flyinge mated indigenous coldblooded stock with many European breeds, most specifically Iberian, Friesian, Barb, and Arab. This produced the breed's foundation stock and a Swedish

Warmblood stud book was eventually opened in 1874. It was necessary for horses to undergo stringent tests before they could be registered to ensure that their conformation was up to standard; action, stamina, temperament, and performance where also rigorously tested.

Over the next 100 years or so, the breed was refined and improved with infusions of Hanoverian, Trakehner, English Thoroughbred, and more Arab. Consequently, it could almost be said that the quality warmblood we know today was especially designed for the purpose, that is, to excel at competition; this includes dressage, eventing, show jumping and carriage-driving.

Appearance: The head is rather fine and long, with a straight nose and a well-defined muzzle with flared nostrils. The ears are long, giving an impression of alertness, and the eyes are

PAGES 212 –215: Originally bred as a cavalry horse, the Swedish Warmblood is now a quality competition horse.

bright and intelligent. The neck is long and elegant with a well-developed crest. The shoulders are muscular and sloping with a good broad chest and deep girth. The back is medium-length with strong loins and well-developed quarters. The long legs are muscular with large joints and the hooves are strong.

Characteristics: These horses are respected for their jumping ability and excellent paces. They are willing, obedient, and intelligent and have a lively and spirited demeanour. In addition to these qualities, they are easy-to-manage and care for and considered hardy and generally healthy.

SWISS WARMBLOOD

Country of Origin: Switzerland

Colors: All solid colors

Height: Around 16 hh

The noble and majestic Swiss Warmblood is based on Switzerland's highly respected Einsiedler breed which dates back at least to the tenth century; in fact, there is evidence that Benedictine monks in Einsiedeln were breeding the horses as early as 1064.

For many centuries the Einsiedler, which is strong and athletic, was used as a riding and driving horse. Gradually, the breed was enhanced when Norman and Hackney blood were added and a little later infusions of Anglo-Norman were also introduced.

It was later, in the twentieth century that the breed really took off when Selle Français and Anglo-Arab were added, making the horse much finer and warmblooded. Then in the 1960s, the Swiss decided that they wanted their own performance and competition horse, so using the remodeled Einsiedler they introduced other European warmbloods such as Hanoverian, Holstein, Trakehner, and Thoroughbred.

The result was the Swiss Warmblood, a high-quality sports horse that excels at dressage, show jumping, and carriage-driving competitions. In its early stages, the National Stud at Avenches used imported stallions, but now that the breed has developed its own standard Swiss Warmbloods are used.

Appearance: The head is of medium size and good quality with a straight or slightly dished nose, intelligent eyes, and alert medium-length ears. The neck is long and elegant with a slight crest. The body is of medium length with a good strong sloping shoulder, broad chest, and deep girth. The legs are long and well developed with well-shaped hooves.

Characteristics: These quality horses are known for their excellent paces and superb jumping ability, having had many successes in international competitions. They are kind, willing, and easy to train.

The Swiss Warmblood is a quality horse with excellent conformation. It has many successes in international competitions, particularly in the disciplines of show jumping and dressage.

TENNESSEE WALKING HORSE

Country of Origin: U.S.A.

Colors: Nearly all colors, but especially black, chestnut, brown, gray, roan, or bay

Height: 15–17 hh

Tennessee Walker (or Plantation) Walking Horse is a breed of gaited horse known for its unique four-beat running-walk and flashy movement. It originated in the deep south of the United States and was recognized as the ideal utility breed to transport plantation owners around their large estates. The smooth, gliding gait of the "Walker" (as the breed is also known) provided hours of comfort in the saddle; the movement is performed from the elbow rather than the shoulder, thus transmitting the minimum of movement to the rider. Although still widely ridden for pleasure, the Walker is nowadays extensively bred for the show ring, and is also used as a general riding and harness horse.

In fact there are two or three characteristic gaits, the flat-footed walk, the running walk, and the canter. The first horse perceived to have this natural talent was foaled in 1837, but it took another 50 years or so to establish the breed as it is today. The Thoroughbred, Standardbred, American Saddlebred, Narragansett Pacer, and Morgan bloodlines all played their part in establishing this distinctive breed, but it was one stallion, foaled in 1886, that became the foundation stallion, possessing all the qualities such as the delightful temperament and the characteristic gaits. Nearly all the offspring inherited their sire's traits and he subsequently enjoyed many successful years at stud. A breed association was established in 1935.

PAGES 218–221: The Tennessee Walking Horse is famous for its unusual gaits. It is now used extensively for pleasure riding.

Appearance: The Walker has a large head with a straight profile, gentle eyes, and pointed ears. The neck is arched and muscular, with a broad base which enables the horse to carry its head high and elegantly. The breed has plenty of bone, which adds to its sturdiness, and has a short-coupled and level topline. The limb joints are well-made, with particularly powerful hocks that allow the hindlegs to step well under the body. The tail is often nicked and set artificially high. It is usually left long.

Characteristics: Walkers are naturally gentle and calm, but it is their unusual gaits for which they are most famous. Although the gaits are inherited they need to be developed by further training. The flat walk, running walk, and canter are natural to the breed. The running walk has several variations: the rack, the stepping pace, the fox-trot, and single-foot.

TERSKY

Country of Origin: Russia

Colors: Predominantly gray, usually with a metallic sheen to the coat. Black, chestnut, and bay are also possible

Height: 15–16 hh

The Tersky or Tersk is a Russian breed of light riding horse of Arab type. It is a true performance horse, specializing in endurance, racing, jumping, and dressage. Not only has it excellent sporting and athletic capabilities, it is also one of the most beautiful of the Russian breeds.

Originating in the northern Caucasus, the breed is now concentrated at the Stavropol Stud. Once, breeding and rearing took place on the steppes, with the result that weaker stock succumbed to wolves or died of disease. Survival of the fittest has consequently made the breed incredibly tough.

The modern breed is a product of the early twentieth century, based on the Strelets Arab, which was produced by crossing Anglo-Arabs with Orlovs, and developed by crossing Arabs with old-type Terskys to which Thoroughbred blood had also been introduced.

There are three variations of Tersky: the first is lightweight, fine and Arab-like in appearance, and is known as the Eastern type. There is also a middleweight, and one that is sturdier and longer in the back, with a frame that is thicker-set. The heavier types have received infusions of Trakehner.

Appearance: The Tersky is a horse of medium height and great beauty, based on Arabian bloodlines which is reflected in its appearance. The head is finely chiselled with a dished profile.

Characteristics: The Tersky has a wonderful temperament. It combines kindness and intelligence with courage and stamina.

The Tersky is one of Russia's finest breeds. It has a good deal of Arab and Thoroughbred in its make up which enhances their capabilities in competitions.

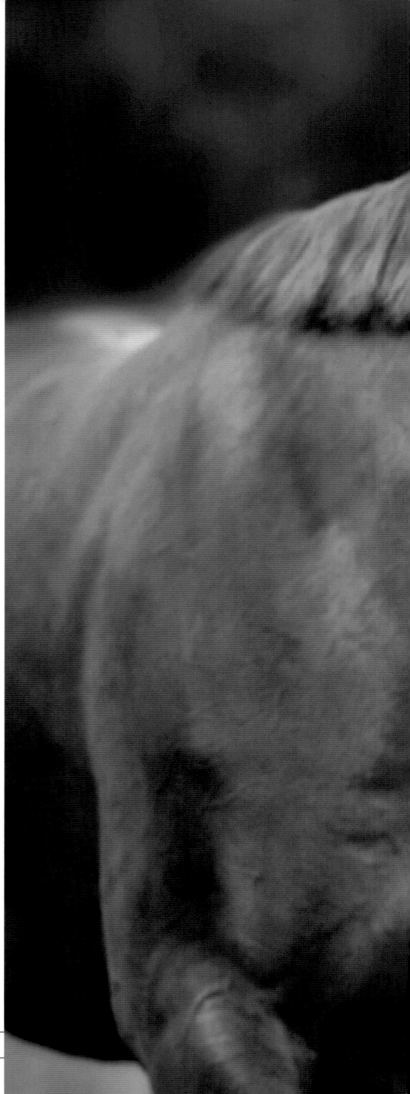

accepted that the modern Thoroughbred stems from three such stallions: the Byerley Turk, the Darley Arabian, and the Godolphin Arabian, all of which had long careers working at stud. Between them, they established the three bloodlines of Herod, Eclipse, and Matchem, which were pivotal to the British Thoroughbred, though the name was not applied to the breed until 1821.

Although initially bred with racing in mind, the qualities of the Thoroughbred make it an ideal horse for all other equestrian disciplines, e.g., eventing, show jumping, dressage, etc. The Thoroughbred has been exported far and wide to improve racing stocks, but has also been used to improve hundreds of other breeds as well.

Thoroughbreds reached the United States in the 1730s— all direct descendants of the three famous foundation stallions, where they were generally similar to those elsewhere; recently, however, a distinctive American type has emerged, with longer hindlegs and longer stride, making its quarters appear higher by comparison.

Appearance: The Thoroughbred is a truly beautiful and athletic animal, with long, clean limbs, a fine, silky coat, an elegant profile, and a muscular body. The eyes are always large and intelligent, the ears finely sculpted. The Thoroughbred is built for stamina and speed.

Characteristics: Thoroughbreds are courageous, honest, and bold. In fact, one has only to watch a steeplechase or hurdle race to see that this is the case. Often the Thoroughbred is described as "hot-headed." While this is probably true of some individuals which may be more sensitive than others, most are a pleasure to own and ride.

TRAKEHNER

Countries of Origin: Germany and Poland

Colors: All solid colors are acceptable

Height: 16–16.2 hh

The Trakehner is the oldest warmblood breed in the world with a history dating back to almost 300 years. It is the most elegant and most Thoroughbred-like of all the warmbloods. Nowadays, because of its athleticism and paces, it is predominantly used for competition, particularly dressage and eventing.

The Trakehner's history is a checkered one dating to 1732 when the first Trakehnen stud was founded in East Prussia, now part of Poland but then in Germany. The stud became the main source of stallions for the whole of Prussia and the area quickly became famous for its beautiful and elegant coach horses.

PAGES 228–233: The Trakehner has a checkered history. Today, it is a popular competition horse, excelling in dressage and eventing.

The Trakehner came into being when native horses of the region were bred with Thoroughbreds and Arabs, infusions which gave it both speed and endurance. Within fifty years, however, the emphasis had shifted from producing coach horses to the breeding of chargers for the cavalry, which continued until World War II, when the Trakehner stud was completely destroyed. Fortunately, towards the end of the war, about 1,000 horses were saved when they were trekked west with refugees escaping from the Russian invasion. Although some of the horses died on the way due to the harsh conditions, sufficient numbers survived to continue the breed. Today, breeding of the Trakehner is again taking place in its place of origin as well as in other countries.

Appearance: In terms of appearance, the Trakehner resembles the middleweight Thoroughbred. The head is fine with an intelligent and interested expression. The profile is straight and similar to that of the Thoroughbred. The neck and shoulders are shapely, the back short and strong, and the quarters powerful. The legs are strong and straight, producing a powerful, straight action.

Characteristics: The Trakehner has an excellent temperament, being amiable, obedient, and courageous. Although it resembles the Thoroughbred, it is without the "hot" temperament associated with that breed. For this reason, breeders looking for an infusion of Thoroughbred without this trait often select Trakehner stallions instead.

UKRAINIAN SADDLE HORSE

Country of Origin: Ukraine

Colors: Most solid colors, particularly bay, chestnut, and black

Height: Up to 16.1 hh

This is a relatively modern breed, in fact, only developed after World War II, formed by crossing Hungarian mares (Nonius, Furioso North Star, Gidrán), with Trakehner, Hanoverian, and Thoroughbred stallions.

The development of the breed was monitored so closely that an extremely useful warmblood was developed in a relatively short space of time, one that was suitable for all disciplines.

Horses are rigorously performance-tested early in their lives before they are sold on, and only the best are retained for breeding purposes.

Appearance: The breed is refined and elegant, its Thoroughbred blood immediately apparent. The eyes are large and bright and the expression intelligent. The profile is straight.

Characteristics: Like most warmbloods, the Ukrainian Saddle or Riding Horse has a kind and obliging nature and a positive attitude to work. It is also courageous and bold.

In its present form the Ukrainian Saddle Horse breed is only around sixty years old. It was bred specifically as a performance horse.

VLADIMIR
HEAVY DRAFT

The Vladimir Heavy Draft has all the fine attributes of a heavy horse, with an alert and proud bearing and lively attitude.

Country of Origin: Russia

Colors: Mainly bay, black, and chestnut

Height: 15.2–16.1 hh

The Vladimir Heavy Draft is a Russian breed of draft horse. It originated at the turn of the twentieth century in the provinces of Vladimir and Ivanovo to the northeast of Moscow.

Local mares were mated with imported heavy breeds, mainly Clydesdales, but were also crossed with Shire, Cleveland Bay, Suffolk Punch, Ardennais, and Percheron. The result is a horse suitable for all heavy draft work.

The breed was officially recognized in 1946 and from then on only horses which satisfied strict conformation criteria and performance tests were registered.

A horse that matures early, the Vladimir Heavy Draft can be put to work and stud when it is three years old.

Appearance: The Vladimir has all the hallmarks of a heavy breed, with a muscular body, broad chest, and strong neck. Its legs are sturdy and well-muscled.

Characteristics: The breed is remarkable for its proud posture and majestic appearance. Unlike some of the other heavy breeds, its paces are forward-going, making it suitable for pulling troikas. Today, the Vladimir is still used for work on farms and in transportation.

THE WELSH BREEDS

Horses were present in Wales as long as 10,000 years ago. The indigenous breed which inhabited the hills was the Celtic Pony and it is thought that all Welsh breeds known today derive from them.

It is recorded that native stock was being bred in Wales in around 50 BC when Julius Caesar founded a stud in Merionethshire and was responsible for introducing Arab blood into the breed. The first mention of Welsh Ponies and Cobs were noted in the laws of Hywel Dda, written in AD 930.

Through the centuries, variations of the original wild ponies were developed. Early on in the twentieth century, the Welsh Pony and Cob Society identified four clear types, described below. These are the original, Welsh Mountain Pony not exceeding 12 hh (Section A); the Welsh Pony not exceeding 13 hh (Section B); the Welsh Pony of Cob Type up to 13.2 hh (Section C); the Welsh Cob of 13.2 –15.2 hh (Section D).

BELOW: Wild Welsh Mountain Ponies on the Isle of Anglesey North Wales, United Kingdom.

RIGHT & PAGES 236–239: Welsh Mountain Ponies.

WELSH MOUNTAIN PONY (SECTION A)

Country of Origin: U.K.

Colors: Mainly gray, but all true colors are acceptable.

Height: Not exceeding 12 hh

The Welsh Mountain Pony is the oldest of all the Welsh breeds. As the name suggests it is tough, resilient, sound in limb as well as constitution. Known for its intelligence, agility, endurance, and hardiness, the Welsh Mountain Pony is capable of surviving the harshest of winters. These ponies are now found all over the world and are highly regarded as quality children's riding ponies.

Appearance: The head is refined, with a small tapering muzzle and small, pricked ears. The eyes are large and bold. These qualities, as well as a dished face, give the Welsh Mountain a distinct resemblance to the Arab. The neck, well-defined withers, and quarters are in proportion to the rest of the pony's body, while the tail is set quite high. The limbs are set square with well-made joints and the feet are small and hard.

Characteristics: The Welsh Mountain is a pony of great personality and charm, having inherited intelligence and quick-wittedness—traits which the original wild ponies seemed to have possessed in abundance. When in action, the gaits must be smooth and the hocks well flexed.

WELSH PONY (SECTION B)

Country of Origin: U.K.

Colors: Mainly gray, but all true colors are acceptable.

Height: Not exceeding 13 hh

The Welsh Pony has all the best attributes of the Welsh Mountain Pony, though breeders have accentuated its talents as a riding pony. Moreover, because the Welsh Pony was used for generations on farms for herding sheep, it is also tough and agile.

These qualities, when combined with good looks, jumping ability, and superb conformation for riding, makes them perfect as children's mounts.

Appearance: The Welsh Pony shares many similarities with the Welsh Mountain Pony. The head is refined, with small pricked ears and the face may be slightly dished. The eyes are large and intelligent. The neck, back, and quarters are muscular and in proportion, with the tail set high. The limbs are straight and strong and the hooves strong and rounded.

Characteristics: The Welsh Pony is willing, active, and enthusiastic and will always give of its best.

The Welsh Pony (Section B) has refined looks combined with strength and toughness. It is an excellent choice for children. Pictured here is a stallion, which is why he has such as large crest.

WELSH PONY OF COB TYPE (SECTION C)

Country of Origin: U.K.

Colors: All true colors are acceptable. For the show ring, however, ponies are preferred with plenty of white on the lower legs.

Height: Not exceeding 13.2 hh

Originally used for farm work, the Welsh Pony of Cob Type was also used for carting slate from the mines. It is the same height as the Welsh Pony, but sturdier and capable of taking the heavier rider. It was developed more as a harness pony than for ridden work and has a naturally pronounced action, probably inherited from the Hackney which was introduced into the breed.

Appearance: The general appearance should be that of a small cob. The eyes are spaced widely apart and the expression is intelligent. Like the other Welsh breeds the ears are small and pricked. The body and legs are sturdier and more cob-like than that of the Welsh Pony, and the feet are also slightly larger. The mane and tail are full.

Characteristics: The Welsh Pony of Cob Type is similar in temperament to the other Welsh breeds, being lively and enthusiastic. It performs well in harness and is also a natural jumper.

WELSH COB
(SECTION D)

Country of Origin: U.K.

Colors: All true colors are acceptable

Height: Not exceeding 13.2 hh–15.2 hh

Of all the Welsh breeds, the Welsh Cob is the most famous. Known for its stunning looks and extravagant paces, it is not only the ultimate working cob, but is also guaranteed to be the center of attention in the show ring.

The breed dates back to the eleventh century when it was known as the Powys Cob or Powys Rouncy. Welsh Cobs not only possess Welsh Mountain Pony blood, they were also influenced by imports from all over the Roman Empire. Breeds from Spain, such as the Andalusian, and the Barb, and Arab from North Africa, were all crossed with the early Welsh Cob variety. Later in the eighteenth and nineteenth centuries other breeds such as Hackney and Yorkshire Coach Horse were also introduced.

Traditionally, Welsh Cobs were used by the military as well as by farmers; they were so versatile that they could be used by anyone needing transport or light haulage.

Appearance: The Welsh Cob is compact, well-muscled, well-balanced, and strong. It has a fine head with large, intelligent eyes, and the usual small, pricked ears. The neck is arched and muscular, the back is short-coupled for strength, and the quarters are powerful and rounded. The legs are sturdy and straight and the feet are in proportion to the animal's body, hard and rounded.

Characteristics: The Welsh Cob is proud, courageous, and extravagant in action. It is suitable for all disciplines.

PAGES 242–245: The Welsh Cob (section D) is very cobby in appearance. It is larger than the other three types and is most striking in appearance with extravagant paces. Its size means that its can be ridden by the whole family.

WESTPHALIAN

Country of Origin: Germany

Colors: All solid colors are acceptable

Height: Not exceeding 15.2 hh–16 hh

The Westphalian is a warmblood horse breed originating in the Westphalia region of western Germany. ike most European warmbloods it is based on an older, heavier breed which was once native to Westphalia for hundreds of years. This native coldblood was bred with Thoroughbred to produce a warmblood which was first registered as a Westphalian in 1826, when the stud book was opened.

For many years, the horse was used for riding and light carriage work until the end of World War II when measures were taken to improve the breed. Westphalian stock was infused with more Thoroughbred and Arab blood to increase its speed and endurance, as well as intelligence. Hanoverian was also used to ensure good sense and obedience.

The result was a superb quality riding horse which first received its true recognition in the 1970s as a competition horse, particularly in show jumping.

Appearance: The head is handsome and broad, with medium wide-apart ears, a straight nose, and clever eyes. The neck is long and well developed with fairly prominent withers, a straight back, strong loins, and well-muscled quarters. The shoulders are sloped with a broad chest and deep girth. The legs are well-proportioned and strong with good bone.

Characteristics: The Westphalian is well-known for its courage and spirit. It is also obedient and easy to handle.

The Westphalian is another German success story, originally bred as a carriage and riding horse. It now excels in dressage, show jumping, and eventing.

WIELKOPOLSKI

Country of Origin: Poland

Colors: All solid colors are acceptable

Height: Not exceeding 15 hh–16.2 hh

The Wielkopolski is a modern breed of horse that originated in central and western Poland. The Wielkopolski shares much of its heritage with the Malopolski, which is another breed of Polish Arab, both originally bred as general riding and driving horses also capable of work on farms. Both are based on native Polish Mazuren and Posnan stock, breeds which now barely exist, having become almost totally subsumed into both the Malopolski and Wielkopolski.

The Wielkopolski was established after World War II when the native stock, which also contained Konik, was bred with Trakehner, Hanoverian, Thoroughbred, and Arab to produce a horse of excellent quality, which was a middleweight used for riding and driving.

There are stringent guidelines to protect the quality of the breed in which all stallions must undergo conformation tests before being allowed to breed.

Appearance: The Wielkopolski has the Arab wedge-shaped head, though it is somewhat plainer. The nose is straight with a neat muzzle and large open nostrils. The ears are medium-length and well-shaped and the eyes are lively and intelligent. The neck is high-set, long, and elegant, with a slight crest. The shoulders are sloping, with a broad chest and a deep girth. The hindquarters are well-muscled, and the legs are long with good bone and well-shaped hooves.

Characteristics: This is a good all-round competition horse also used for driving. It is strong with plenty of stamina and endurance, used on farms and for light draft work in its native land. It has a kind and quiet temperament and is a willing and obedient worker.

The Wielkopolski makes a first class competition horse because of its temperament, comfortable gaits, and hardiness. It excels show jumping, dressage, and eventing.

Chapter Three
HORSE IN THE WILD

Throughout much of history, mankind's encounters with horses, have been with the domesticated kind, for the horse has lived in our company for thousands of years. Once used as warhorses, as beasts of burden, and for transporting human beings, the horse's modern-day purpose seems to be solely for our pleasure, all of which are a far cry from its true evolution as a wild, free-roaming herd animal.

Instinctively companionable and highly gregarious, horses are at their most content with others of their kind, surrounded by plenty of open space and unhindered by fencing, so it is hardly surprising that once freedom is allowed they should revert to natural behavior. In the wild, horses form themselves into a herd, with a dominant stallion as their leader, which protects its group of mares and youngsters. The herd forms a close unit, its members playing, grooming, feeding, and resting together, all the while keeping a watchful eye for signs of danger. During the mating season, the stallion will fight for herd dominance, securing for itself plenty of breeding females in the process.

Horses have evolved to be perfectly adapted to living in the open. They are powerful sprinters capable of achieving significant speeds when fleeing from danger. They have large eyes, set on the sides of their heads, which provide almost all-round vision. They also have extremely good hearing, and their mobile, pointed ears allow them to catch sounds from all angles.

The instinct to herd provides the group with relative safety compared with that of a lone animal; a galloping group tends to confuse would-be predators, while any animal that is brought down would more likely be one that is weak or sick.

The term "wild horse" is also used colloquially to refer to free-roaming herds of feral horses such as the Mustang in the United States, the Brumby in Australia, and many others. These feral horses are untamed members of the domestic horse subspecies (*Equus ferus caballus*) and should not be confused with the two truly "wild" horse subspecies, the Tarpan or Eurasian Wild Horse (*Equus ferus ferus*), once native to Europe and western Asia, and Przewalski's Horse (*Equus ferus przewalskii*).

BRUMBY

Country of Origin: Australia

Colors: All solid colors, dun, roan, and pinto

Height: Up to 15 hh

The Brumby is a free-roaming feral horse in Australia. They were introduced during the country's gradual colonization, and in particular by settlers who arrived during the nineteenth-century gold rush. Before then, Australia had no native horses of her own. There was not only an influx of people, therefore, but of animals, and this included the horses which they brought with them. During World War I, many of the horses escaped or were turned loose to run wild: these were the forefathers of the modern-day Brumby, a name said to be derived from the aboriginal word for wild (baroomby).

Appearance: Due to the variety of animals which reverted to a wild state, there is no specific breed type; consequently Brumbies come in all shapes, sizes, and colors.

Characteristics: The horses are now almost totally feral, making them difficult to catch and almost impossible to train. They are prolific breeders and for this reason have come to be regarded as pests. This has led to such extensive culling that they are now quite rare.

PAGES 251–253: The Brumby was introduced to Australia by settlers who turned the horses loose and let them run wild.

CAMARGUE

Country of Origin: France

Colors: Usually gray, occasionally bay and brown

Height: 13.1–14.2 hh

The Camargue is an ancient breed of horse indigenous to the salt marshes and lagoons of the Rhône delta in southeast France. They are semi-wild and spend much of their time grazing the sparse vegetation. Their origin is relatively unknown, although they are probably descended from the Diluvial Horse. They also bear a striking resemblance to the primitive horses painted in the caves at Lascaux in prehistoric times; it is also likely that they are related to Oriental and Barb because of their facial shape.

The breed was further enhanced in the nineteenth century by the introduction of Postier Breton, Arab, Anglo-Arab, and Thoroughbred, though these additions seem to have had little bearing on the horses' overall appearance.

There is an annual round-up in the Camargue when suitable horses are selected for riding purposes while the weaker and substandard colts and stallions are culled: this may seem ruthless but there is no doubt that it has led to improvements in the breed.

Camargue horses are traditionally ridden by the *gardians* who use them for herding the famous black bulls of the region and for festivals in which their dazzling horsemanship is displayed. The horses are also used for trekking the region, now a popular tourist attraction.

Appearance: The head is slightly square, with a broad forehead, short, broad ears, and expressive eyes. The neck is short and well-developed, the shoulder is upright, and the back is short with a low-set tail. The legs are strong and the hooves well-shaped and tough. The mane and tail are abundant.

Characteristics: Camargues make obedient and willing riding horses; they are extremely agile and have the ability to turn sharply at full gallop. They are sure-footed and have plenty of stamina. Interestingly, when they are trained, they never quite lose their independent and wild spirit.

PAGES 254–257: Camargue Horses inhabit the salt marshes and lagoons of the Rhône delta. It is thought that they are descended from the Diluvial horse.

KONIK

Country of Origin: Poland

Colors: Usually light-brown or dun and sometimes bay. The mane and tail are full and the dorsal stripe and zebra markings are sometimes visible.

Height: 12.2–13.3 hh

The Konik is a small, semi-feral horse originating in Poland. The word konik derives from *koń*, the Polish word for horse. The Konik resembles the wild Tarpan of eastern Europe and western Asia which is now extinct. The Konik itself is not a specific breed and there is no particular standard. However, there are around five types, some with native blood and others with Arab added.

The Konik, being related to the Tarpan, which was a small horse of Oriental origin, has a small, neat head, dorsal stripe, and zebra markings. Sadly, the last remaining Tarpan died in captivity in 1887, having been hunted to extinction some ten years earlier.

In the last century, efforts were made to revive the ancient breed by preserving the Konik's Tarpan genes. These reconstituted Tarpans, as they are now known, live wild in a nature reserve where they are beginning to manifest many Tarpan characteristics. Today, Koniks are mainly used for farm work and occasionally as children's ponies.

Appearance: A strong head with great character that shows its Oriental origins. The neck is of medium length and quite thick but with a good carriage. The body is stout and sturdy with medium-length legs with good bone, which are slightly feathered. The hooves are tough.

Characteristics: The Konik is hardy and will live out all year round with little extra feeding and care. Some can be willful and difficult—a throwback to their wild Tarpan origins.

PAGES 258–261: The Konik is the closest relative to the now extinct Tarpan. Attempts have been made to preserve the Tarpan gene-pool which is present in the breed.

MUSTANG

Country of Origin: U.S.A.

Colors: Any color, but mainly brown, chestnut, bay, dun, and pinto

Height: 14–16 hh

The Mustang is a free-roaming horse of America's West. They descended from horses brought to the Americas by the *conquistadores*. Although horses were once present in North America, by the time the Spanish arrived in the sixteenth century, the original prehistoric horses had long been extinct. The Spanish brought Iberian horses with them in their ships, derived mainly from Arabs and Barbs, and many of these sleek, desert-bred, and resilient horses were allowed to wander off, spreading into North America and forming feral herds in their new environment.

Native American tribes came to value the Mustang's qualities and many were caught and domesticated by them. They even developed their own breeds based on the Mustang, such as the Appaloosa, the Cayuse Indian Pony,

PAGES 262–265: The Mustang's ancestors are horses that came over with the conquistadors; *many were turned loose and formed the basis of the breed as it is today.*

and the Chickasaw Indian Pony, also known as the Florida Cracker Horse.

By the beginning of the nineteenth century, there were between one- and two-million Mustangs in existence, many of which ran free, but others were domesticated and used by settlers. Unfortunately, the wild horses were regarded as pests and were culled by the thousands to make room for cattle. But it wasn't only the ranchers who were responsible for the decimation of the population. Thousands were killed in the twentieth century, sacrificed to the pet-food industry.

Sadly, there are less than 50,000 Mustangs in existence today and in some areas numbers are dangerously low. Determined efforts are now being made to safeguard the breed for the future and, fortunately for the Mustang, the breed is now considered an important part of the American heritage and a protected species.

Appearance: Mustangs come in all colors, sizes, and builds, although horses which display Barb characteristics are most favored by breeders.

Characteristics: The Mustang is easy to train, due to its intelligence. Natural selection in the wild has made the breed particularly tough and resilient.

PRZEWALSKI'S HORSE

Country of Origin: Mongolia

Colors: Various shades of dun, ranging from yellow to red. They have black manes and tails and black legs, often with zebra markings. There is a black dorsal stripe running down the back. The muzzle and surrounding the eyes is creamy white

Height: 12–14 hh

Native to the steppes of central Asia, this is a truly ancient breed, also known as the Mongolian or Asiatic Wild Horse. The Przewalski is stocky and dun-colored with a dark-brown erect mane. Primitive horses of this kind were hunted by man 20,000 years ago and the likenesses of similar horses can be seen in prehistoric cave paintings in Spain and France. Until recently, it was almost certainly extinct in the wild, as no sightings of it have been made for over 30 years, it is the only true wild equine and the ancestor of the domestic horse.

The earliest written evidence of its existence was in the ninth century and later in 1226 when a herd of wild horses were supposed to have caused Genghis Khan, of the Mongol Empire, to fall from his horse.

Due to its isolation and the fierceness with which stallions protect their mares, the Mongolian horse's bloodline remained pure and can be traced back to its primitive ancestors. It gets its modern name from the man who brought it to the attention of the world, Colonel N.M. Przewalski, a Polish explorer, who acquired the remains of a wild horse in 1881 from hunters who

PAGES 266–269: The Przewalski's Horse has been re-introduced into the wild in Mongolia, China, and Russia.

had discovered them in the Gobi Desert of western Mongolia. He took them to the zoological museum in St. Petersburg where naturalist I.S. Poliakoff examined them and decided that they belonged to a species of primitive wild horse. Following the discovery, some of the living horses were captured and kept in captivity in zoos, in order to save them from total extinction.

The captive population has increased rapidly and is carefully monitored at Prague Zoo, which holds the stud book of the breed. The horses are kept in as natural conditions as possible and some have been released back into the wild in China, Russia, and Mongolia, where they are a protected species; there is also a successful population in France.

Appearance: The head is of medium size with a broad forehead and a straight or slightly dished nose. The eyes are set high on the head and are rather small with a wild look. The nose tapers to a narrow muzzle with small low-set nostrils. The body is strong, with a longish, straight back, a thick, short neck, and weak quarters. The legs are short and stocky with hard, tough hooves.

Characteristics: Przewalskis are never tamed and can be aggressive and ferocious, especially in the presence of their young. They need little care as they are extremely hardy.

Chapter Four
MARES, FOALS, AND STALLIONS

MARES

A mare is a term used for most female equines including the horse. However, one exception is a female donkey that is known as a jenny. A mare will become sexually mature by the age of two, which means that at this age she is able to mate and produce offspring. She will usually come into season in the late spring or early summer. This is when she is ready to be covered by a stallion. Once the foal has been conceived, the mare will carry her foal for around eleven months. This gestation period invariably results in the foal being born in the

PAGES 270–273: Mares carry their foals for approximately eleven months from conception to birth.

following spring or early summer. This is nature's way of ensuring that the foal is born in warm conditions and when food is most plentiful. At this time of year, the grass is at its best. This will enable the mare to produce the best quality milk for her foal.

A mare that is kept exclusively for breeding purposes is called a broodmare. She is usually a horse with a good bloodline and a reputation for producing good, healthy, and strong foals. Sometimes, a broodmare has had a previous proven career in racing or competition.

If a mare is kept for leisure or competition purposes, it is unlikely that her owner will allow her the time off to have a foal. However, for an owner who would love to experience the whole process of allowing their mare to have a foal, they will have to be committed to giving their mare a good deal of time off for the whole process.

Some mares used for top competition can still technically breed. This is done by embryo transfer (ET), that is the technique of removing an embryo from the uterus of one mare—the biological dam—and placing it in the uterus of a recipient mare. The recipient carries the fetus, delivers the foal, and nurses it until weaning. This allows high-class mares to continue their competitive careers while producing foals, or for the breeding of more than one foal from a mare each season. ET first emerged in the 1970s and has become increasingly popular over the past 10 years.

A foal bonds with his mother within the first few hours of life. At times when he is feeling anxious, he will stay close to her side.

FOALS

Everyone who loves horses also loves a foal!

When the mare has been pregnant for around twenty-three days, the foal's heartbeat can be heard for the first time. By 150 days the placenta is fully formed around the embryo. After eleven months, the mare will go into labor. It is quite normal for the mare to give birth fairly quickly, often within an hour. In the wild, a mare in the process of giving birth is extremely vulnerable to predators, so giving birth quickly is nature's way of keeping danger to a minimum. A mare will usually lie down to give birth, but can also do it standing up. Once born, the foal will be vigorously licked by its mother to encourage it to take its first breath and stimulate its circulation. The foal will be on its feet and suckling from its mother within minutes and will be able to run around within hours. The male foal is called a colt and the female a filly.

The foal will start to take an interest in grain and grass within a couple of weeks of birth. Sometimes, it will even attempt to eat while lying down, as standing up can be a tricky thing for a foal to do as its legs are very long compared with its neck. However, despite attempts to eat these food sources, foals are reliant on their mother's milk for the first few months of their lives. By around four to six months though, the foal will be largely eating solid food as its mother's milk can no longer sustain it.

Like all young animals, foals are lively and playful, but in the early months, they will not venture far, staying close to the mare, learning from her and the other horses in the vicinity.

Young horses grow rapidly in their first year reaching around 90 percent of their adult height and around 80 percent of their adult weight.

In the wild, as a foal matures, it will gradually leave its mother to spend more and more time with the other young horses in the herd, eventually becoming independent.

A foal is horse under one year old. To be more specific, a filly is a female foal and a colt is a male foal.

However, domesticated foals have to be weaned from their mothers artificially. This means that they are separated forcefully, so that the foal can gain independence, and the mare can be brought back into riding work or breed again. Weaning can be stressful for the mare and the foal, so this is a task that should only be undertaken by those who are experienced in the process. Weaning is usually carried out when the foal is six months old. On reaching the age of one, it is called a yearling.

Horses in the wild give birth naturally in the spring and early summer. However, domesticated horses are often encouraged to mate and give birth earlier. This is very much the case for horses bred for racing. It is preferred that foals are born to as near to January 1 as possible. In the southern hemisphere, the preferred date for birth is August 1. This manipulation of nature is designed to give a horse an advantage when competing, particularly in races. The earlier in the year they were born, the stronger and more mature they are.

PAGES 278–281: Foals under human management are weaned between four and six months of age.

STALLIONS

The term "stallion" dates from the era of Henry VII, who passed a number of laws relating to the breeding and export of horses in an attempt to improve the British stock. A stallion is a male horse who is capable of mating with a mare to produce offspring. They are largely kept at stud farms for reproduction purposes. Stallions require specialized handling as they can be undisciplined and strong-willed at times. To complicate matters further, they cannot be kept with other horses for they have a tendency to fight with other males or attempt to mate with females. For this reason, many stallions are often stabled for much of the day. If they are lucky enough to be able to be kept at grass, they require plenty of security and high and safe fencing to prevent them from jumping out. However, despite the temperaments of some, stallions can be wonderful to own and very loyal. They can be used for a number of purposes, including trail riding, racing, show jumping, dressage, and eventing. For those wishing to keep a stallion, it is vital that the owner is specially trained in their care, for they can become a handful if not taught discipline. Stallions are sexually mature around three but are capable of mating as young as one.

PAGES 282–285: Stallions must be trained to behave with respect toward humans at all times, as they can be aggressive.